The Santa Claus Book

The Santa Claus Book

E. Willis Jones

WALKER AND COMPANY
New York

Contents

Copyright © 1976 by E. Willis Jones

See page 127, which constitutes an extension of this copyright page.

First published in the United States of America in 1976 by the Walker Publishing Company, Inc.

Published simultaneously in Canada by Fitzhenry & Whiteside, Limited, Toronto.

Design concept, E. Willis Jones
Project designer, Marsha Picker

ISBN: 0–8027–0541–3

Library of Congress Catalog Card Number: 76–13817

Printed in the United States of America.

10 9 8 7 6 5 4 3 2 1

Preface

Yes, there is a Santa Claus. And as a newspaper editor reassured a wavering eight-year-old Virginia O'Hanlon in 1897: "He exists as certainly as love and generosity and devotion exist, and you know that they abound and give to your life its highest beauty and joy."

The editor might have informed his eight-year-old correspondent that there is also a St. Nicholas, San Nicola, Sancte Claus, Hoteiosho, Père Noël, Father Christmas, Sinterklaas, Sonnerklas, and many more. Whatever the name, the origin of each region's Santa can be traced to the youthful Bishop Nicholas of Myra in Asia Minor who gave gifts and wrought miracles for boys and girls—and grown-ups—some 1,700 years ago.

But before we trace the story of Santa Claus at Christmas, consider the meaning of that day. First of all, it is the celebration of the birth of the Christ child at Bethlehem. To most of us it also means other beautiful things: remembrance of Christmases past, of family love and joy, of the pleasurable appeals to our senses of taste and smell (that Christmas dinner in the making), of hearing and sight—in carols and hymns, the decorated tree, the holly and mistletoe. Christmas promotes feelings of brotherhood, goodwill, faith, and renewed hope for everlasting peace. Not least, it is a time to taste the joy of giving, as exemplified by the miraculous arrival of Santa Claus and his sleigh over the rooftops. For hundreds of millions the world over Santa represents the very spirit of Christmas and a merry reminder of all the good things that Christmas means.

Although always a benefactor over 1,700 years, St. Nicholas has been regarded a jolly and hearty fellow for only the past century and a half. And this transformation into the Santa Claus we know today was made at the hands of American writers and illustrators.

Whether St. Nicholas or Santa, his story is essentially a happy one, although he has had some strife and scroogelike detractors along the way, as we shall see.

1 Everyone's St. Nicholas

St. Nicholas, as bishop, holds three golden balls symbolizing the three dowries. On his robe are events in the life of Christ. Painted by Gentile da Fabriano in 1425.

The Boy Nicholas

Our story begins around A.D. 270 along the northern shores of the Mediterranean Sea in a country called Lycia, today a small part of Turkey. About 350 miles southeastward across the sea, then often a week's journey by ship, is the birthplace of Jesus. Christianity had been brought to Lycia and the surrounding lands by that most traveled of the apostles, Paul, only a little over two centuries earlier.

At the western edge of the town of Patara and near the sea was a fine house behind which rolled rich farm lands. It was the home of a most devout couple, Epyhanus and his wife, Johane. Though comfortable in wordly goods, they nevertheless felt poor, because in their thirty years of marriage, no children had come to enrich their lives.

But then, as if in answer to their many prayers, a boy was born to them, and the event itself was widely hailed as a miracle. The baby was named Nicholas, meaning *victorious*. It is said of him that, when first bathed in a tub, he stood up and raised his arms—as if praising God—and then proceeded to refuse to take milk from his mother until after sundown on Wednesdays and Fridays, the fasting days of the Church.

Aside from these unusual acts, his boyhood was a normal and happy one until his ninth year, when both of his parents died during a plague that swept the land. The early accounts tell how he transferred the great love he had for his mother and father to the poor and needy of the little town, and his guardians did not restrain this love, which was expressed in good deeds such as giving away food, clothing, and sometimes money—always in secret and usually at night.

One such legend that has come down through the ages tells of an elderly nobleman, a former friend of Nicholas's parents, who had three lovely daughters but had lost all his wealth. Each maiden had a suitor, but custom dictated that no girl would be taken in marriage unless provided with a suitable dowry by her family. So, without telling their father, the girls

In Saint Nicholas Providing Dowries, *by Lorenzo di Bicci (1375-1452), an elongated Nicholas has been given a halo prematurely, since he is said to have helped the three maidens when only a young lad.*

had decided to draw lots to see which one would offer herself for sale on the town auction block (meaning that she would enter into prostitution) to provide dowries for the other two.

When word of their plight reached Nicholas, he waited only for the cover of night before proceeding to their house, where he lowered a small bag of gold through the open window of the eldest girl's room. Whether or not it actually fell into a stocking hanging there to dry, as some tales have it, is not known, but in any case she was soon married. On other dark nights, the same act of kindness was repeated for the other two daughters—with equally happy results. On the third occasion a noise brought the father to his window just in time to see that it was Nicholas who had saved the family from disgrace. With gratitude in his heart, he kept the secret safe for many years.

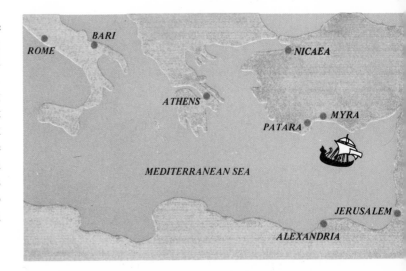

A Sinking Ship Saved

To further Nicholas's religious training, his guardians arranged for him to visit the Holy Land. The sea journey was a thrilling experience for the young man still in his teens, and when he arrived in Jerusalem he marveled at the sights and sounds that he found there.

Although his studies and his explorations of the Holy City absorbed him wholly, he felt called to return to his own homeland, and so Nicholas once again put out to sea. It was this return voyage that set the course his life would follow.

They were not yet in sight of land when a great storm engulfed them, and it was to the young traveler

7

The Golden Legend,
*originally a French and Latin
compilation of the lives of the
saints, was translated and
printed by the great William
Caxton, first English printer,
in 1483. The title page is
below; at **right** is one of the
text pages.*

*A sixteenth-century French
woodcut (**opposite below**) also
depicts the saint saving the
lives of three schoolboys. The
most frequently portrayed of all
the saint's miracles, the revived
"schoolboys" have been
portrayed as ranging in age
from infants to grown men.*

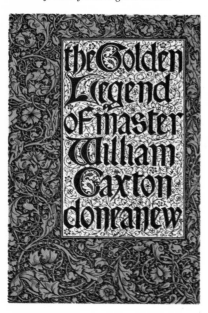

Of the Lyf
of Seynt
Nicholas
the Bisshop

one hys neyhbour had thenne thre doughters, virgyns, and he was a noble man, but for the pouerte of them to gydre they were constrayned and in veray purpose to abandonne theym to the synne of lecherye, so that by the gayne and wynnyng of their infamye he myght be susteyned. ℂ And whan the holy man Nycholas knewe herof he had grete orrour of thys vylonye, and threwe by nyght secretly in to the hows of the man a masse of golde wrapped in a cloth. And whan the man aroos in the mornyng he fonde this masse of gold, and rendred to god therfor grete thanknges, & therwith he maryed hys oldest doughter. And a lityl whyle after thys holy seruaunt of god threwe in an other masse of gold whyche the man fonde, and thanked god, and purposed to wake for to knowe hym that so had ayded hym in hys pouerte. And a fewe dayes Nicholas doubled the masse of gold and caste it in to the hows of this man. ℂ He awoke by the sowne of the gold and folowed Nicholas whiche fledde fro hym & he said to hym, Syre flee not away so but that I may see and knowe the. Thenne he ran after hym more hastely and knewe that it was Nicholas, and anon he kneled doun & wold haue kyssed hys feet, but the holy man wold not, but requyred hym not to telle ne descouer thys thyng as longe as he lyued.

AFTER thys the bysshop of the cyte of Myrre deyde & other bysshoppis assembled for to pourueye to this chyrche a bysshop. And ther was emong the other a bysshop of grete auctoryte, and alle the lectyon was in hym. And whan he had warned all for to be in fastynges and in prayers, thys bysshop herd that nyght a voys whiche said to hym that at houre of matyns he shold take hede to the dores of the chyrche, and hym that shold come first to the chirche and haue the name of Nicholas, they shold sacre hym bysshop. ℂ And he shewid this to the other bysshops and admonested them for to be alle in prayers. And he kepte the dores. And this was a merueyllous thyng, for atte hour of matyns lyke as he had be sent fro god, Nicholas aroos to fore all other. And the bysshop toke hym whan he was comen and demanded of hym hys name. And he whyche was symple as a douue enclyned hys heed and said, I haue to name Nicholas. Thenne the bysshop said to hym ℂ Nicholas seruaunt and frende of god, for your holynes ye shal be bysshop of this place. And syth they brought hym to the chyrche, how be it that he refused it strongly, yet they sette hym in the chayer. And he folowed as he dyde to fore in all thynges of humylyte and honeste of maners. He woke in prayers and made hys body lene, he eschiewed companye of wymen, he was humble in receyuyng all thynges, prouffytable in spekyng, joyous in admonestyng, and cruel in correctyng.

that the sailors turned for reassurance that they would survive. For two days and two nights Nicholas prayed for their safety, while the ship tossed and rolled on heavy seas. Then, at dawn on the third day, they found themselves near the safe harbor of Myra, a city not far distant from his birthplace. When they landed to make repairs, Nicholas's first thought was

to find the quiet of a church to thank God for their deliverance.

It so happened that the bishop of the district had recently died, and high-ranking clergy were conferring in that same church to select his successor. At the close of the previous day, one candidate had seemed to stand out as the logical choice, but it had

*In the miracle of the replenished grain ships (**above**), the bishop Nicholas saved his people from starvation. For good measure, the painter Fra Angelico (c.1445) included a storm-tossed ship being saved by the saint from the sky.*

been agreed that the decision would be held over until the next morning. Then, as told in the medieval manuscript, THE GOLDEN LEGEND:

". . . this bishop heard that night a voice which said to him that, at the hour of matins . . . him that should first come to the church and have the name Nicholas they should declare him bishop. And he spoke this to the other bishops and admonished them to be all in prayers. And he kept the doors. And this was a marvellous thing, for at the hour of matins, like as he had been sent from God, Nicholas rose before all others . . . and the bishop told him of what was coming . . . and how be it that he refused it strongly, yet they set him in the chair."

Other accounts say he then attended the monastery in a nearby town, completing his training before becoming the abbot of the order and then bishop of the district.

Though young, the new bishop was loved and respected by his people. So many legends about his miracles have been handed down—by word of mouth or in manuscript—and with so many variations that it is difficult to tell which may be closest to the original (see "The Twenty-one Miracles" p. 14).

Saint Nicholas Resuscitating the Three Youths *(above)*, *a painting by Lorenzo di Bicci, is a companion to the di Bicci on page 7. Originally in a monastery in Florence, the pair are now at the Metropolitan Museum of Art in New York.*

*An old French hand-colored print (**opposite**) shows the innkeeper butchering the three boys and the saint simultaneously saving them.*

*Another version of the miracle of the three boys (**below**), who are unusually mature in this painting by Francisco Pesselino (1422-1457).*

The Young Bishop and Three Boys

The tale of the miracle of the three schoolboys has many variations. One has them returning home for the holidays from a boarding school and stopping overnight at an inn where they were held, presumably for ransom, by the rascally innkeeper. Appealed to by the boys' worried parents, the young bishop searched the road until he came to the inn, where the villain finally admitted he had put the boys into pickling casks. With a wave of his sceptre, Nicholas caused the boys to step forth from the casks alive and well. A more popular version has it that the boys had been butchered, then readily reassembled at the bishop's bidding.

Many miracles are recorded for the years he was a bishop, but one that occurred just after his elevation to Archbishop of all Lycia was to be particularly important to the fame of St. Nicholas as gift-giver and provider.

Bad weather had caused a great shortage of food, particularly grains, and there was widespread fear of famine. Several ships carrying grain from Constantinople to Alexandria had sought refuge from a storm in the harbor of Myra. With some difficulty, Nicholas succeeded in persuading the ships' captains that if they provided the region with a year's supply of grain, their hoppers would nonetheless be full upon reaching their destination. This act saved his people, and when the prediction proved to be true at the end of the voyage captains and sailors spread word far and wide. To this feat is ascribed his later adoption as patron saint by so many cities all over the world.

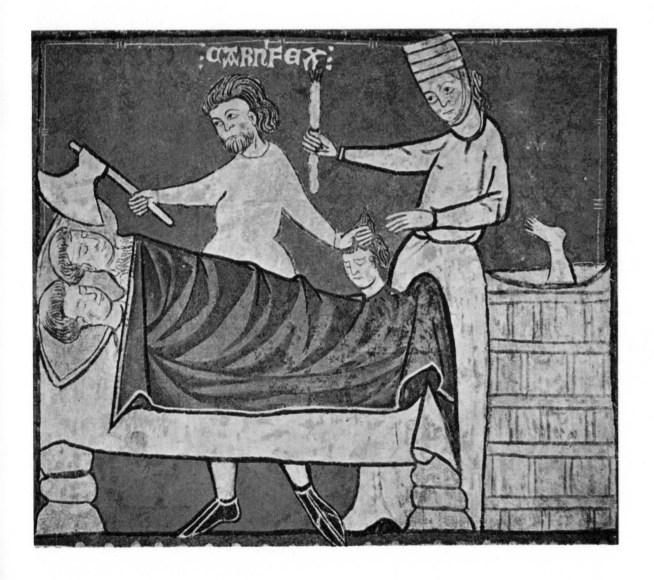

The consecration of young Nicholas as Bishop of Myra c.300 A.D. is interpreted 1,200 years later by the French painter, Jehan Fouquet.

The Miraculous Bishop

As time went on, legends of the good bishop's deeds on land and sea became abundant. But the records also show a stormy side to his life. Twice he found himself in prison. The first occasion, when he was in his early fifties, came from his resisting the widespread persecutions of Christians ordered by the Roman Emperors of that time. Although tortured for many months, perhaps as long as three years, his faith held firm and he was released to his joyful people when Constantine the Great became the first Christian ruler of the Roman Empire. The second imprisonment was brief. At the First Council of Nicaea (in Byzantium) in A.D. 325, Emperor Constantine had called all the bishops of the Christian world to resolve important points on theological questions. In heated debate Bishop Nicholas slapped a fellow bishop in the face and was put in a cell overnight to cool off. The next morning, having been miraculously unshackled during the night, he returned to the council chamber, and his point soon prevailed.

After nearly fifty years as the beloved spiritual leader of his people, Nicholas died on the sixth day of December, probably in the year A.D. 343. His people called it his "Birthday in Heaven" and built an elaborate crypt for his remains in the church at Myra. Partially restored, the church still stands in the town that is now known as Demre, Turkey.

Within two hundred years this church bore the name, Church of St. Nicholas, the first of many hundreds of churches to be so named around the world. In the telling and retelling of his miracles and legends, it is small wonder that the boy Nicholas of Patara had become the universally revered St. Nicholas of Myra. The recognition of his sainthood was a popular process taking place well before the formal procedures of canonization had become established.

With his spreading fame he soon would become the patron of new towns, cities, and countries, ships, and many diverse groups: sailors, and quite naturally, schoolboys and maidens (spinsters would appeal to St. Nicholas to gain husbands), and pawnbrokers, who in time changed those three bags of gold, as had artisans of the Middle Ages, into three golden balls, which became the saint's symbol when portrayed by painters during the Renaissance.

12

St. Nicholas rescues a foundering ship and its distressed crew in this richly illuminated manuscript page from The Book of Hours *of Jean, Duke of Berry.*

13

Twenty-one Miracles

Many early manuscripts tell of Nicholas as bishop, saint, and miracle maker, most being copied from writings of three ecclesiastics of the ninth and tenth centuries. The earliest was by Methodius, bishop of Constantinople from 842 to 846, whose works were finally put into print in Naples, 1751, as *S. Nicolai Acta Primigenia*. Next in importance was one written before 872 by Johannes Diaconus, a Neopolitan ecclesiastic whose writings were among the earliest known; this manuscript was published in Naples in 1479 as *Vitae Sanctorum*. The third was by Simeon Metaphrastes, who ventured some added miracles in the early part of the tenth century.

The twenty-one miracles that are generally credited to Nicholas have been recorded in a poem written about 1150 by Wace, or Guace, a Norman who became chief of scribes to the French royal house. His poem was written for metrical sermons, as was the custom, and for the first time the tales were told so as to be understood by the average person. Six of the most frequently repeated miracles have already been noted: religious acts in infancy; dowries for the three maidens; being chosen bishop; saving the three schoolboys; saving ship and sailors from storm; providing grain during famine.

Wace's poem was nearly 1500 lines long, but here, briefly are the other fifteen miracles:

● In the excitement of going to see her archbishop, a woman left her baby in a tub of water over a fire. Remembering, she appealed to Nicholas and the baby was found unhurt, playing in the bubbling water.

● A child, so afflicted by a demon as to be uncontrollable, was brought to the bishop who drove out the demon and healed the child.

● The pagan goddess, Diana, angered by the bishop's interference with her adulation, appeared as a nun to sailors who were headed for Myra. She asked them to take a gift of "holy oil" to the bishop for annointing the steps and walls of the new church. But Nicholas instructed the sailors to throw it out on the sea, whereupon it burst into flames.

● Three noblemen, unjustly sentenced to death by the emperor of Constantinople, prayed to the saint who then appeared in a dream, threatening the court's annihilation if the prisoners were not set free. The noblemen were not only freed by the converted monarch but offered gifts as well.

● The saint healed great numbers of the sick and freed many from evil spirits.

● From the saint's tomb came a continuous flow of oil with magical powers for healing.

● An archbishop was unjustly exiled by the ruler of the land, whereupon the oil ceased to flow from the saint's tomb. When he was reinstated, the oil flowed again.

● A pagan who had crossed the sea to rob Christians found an image of St. Nicholas and was told it would protect his ill-gotten gains. However, thieves stole his loot, so he struck the image of the saint. Nevertheless, the saint saw to it that the monies were returned, and both robber and thieves were converted to Christianity.

● A Christian borrowed money from a Jew and pledged repayment on the image of St. Nicholas. When the debt was due, he declared he had paid it. The Jew said he would consider the debt satisfied if, at their next meeting, the debtor would swear on the saint's image that the money had been returned. On the day of the meeting the Christian enclosed the money due in a walking stick and asked the Jew to hold it while he took the oath. Retrieving the stick, he started homeward only to be struck by a cart, which broke the stick and exposed the fraud. The Jew got his money, the Christian was returned to health and integrity, and the Jew's entire household was converted.

A particularly gruesome rendering of the three-boy legend is this eighteenth-century French print.

● Fulfilling a vow, a man had a costly cup made to offer at the saint's tomb. Then, considering it too beautiful to give, he had a cheaper one made. With his wife and son he went on a pilgrimage to Myra, and on the voyage his son, while holding the finer cup, fell overboard. At the church, the bereaved father laid the second cup on the altar, but it repeatedly fell off. The repentant father confessed, causing the son with the finer cup to come running to him.

● A long-married couple made a pilgrimage to Myra to pray for a son. Their prayers were answered. The child, who was born on St. Nicholas Day, was later stolen and sold to the Saracen emperor and grew up in his service. Every December 6 the couple prayed for his return until finally their prayers were answered. Their son was returned to them on St. Nicholas Day.

● While sleeping at an inn, a merchant on a pilgrimage to the church at Myra was killed by the innkeeper, his mangled remains put into a barrel. The saint came, restored the merchant to life, and left in the night. The next morning the innkeeper, in fear and amazement, joined the merchant on his pilgrimage.

● A man of Lombardie celebrated the saint's feast day annually. On one such occasion, his young daughter was left alone in the house. The devil appeared at the door disguised as a beggar asking for bread and strangled the little girl. Then, after the father had returned, St. Nicholas appeared at the door disguised as a pilgrim asking for bread. The father showed him the child's body, and she was soon brought back to life.

● A baron-pilgrim, wishing to take back to his country a relic of the saint, made off with a tooth. Through its wrappings came a steady flow of oil. Then, after the saint appeared to the baron in a dream saying that his body must not be divided, he awoke to find the tooth gone.

● A paralytic who could not even raise his hand was carried to the monastery of the saint, who annointed him with holy oils and prayed—and he was healed.

☐

*A fine example of a Russian conception of the miracle maker is seen in this seventeenth-century mosaic icon (**left**).*

*The Church of St. Nicholas at Myra (**above**) had fallen into ruins by the nineteenth century. It was restored by the Russians, who added an upper story and tower. It is now preserved as a museum by the government of Turkey.*

*The saint's elaborate crypt at Myra (**opposite left**) was broken into in A.D. 1087 by Norman sailors who took many of the relics to Bari, Italy. The remaining relics are to this day in the church at Myra (**opposite right**).*

The Saint's Travels Begin

In their declining years sailors of the Mediterranean and the North Atlantic often became boatmen on the calm rivers, and they took their saint with them as they journeyed inland up and down the valleys of the Scheldt, Meuse, Moselle, Rhine, Rhone, Danube, and the other major rivers of Europe.

What is now Belgium became the first western region to fully accept St. Nicholas, not only by building a shrine on the Scheldt River near Antwerp, but also by giving his name to both a church and the nearby city of Saint Nicholas. In addition, many tradesmen

took him as patron—dyers, wood-turners, seedsmen, packers, coopers, even haberdashers. And during the next few hundred years nearly all the river towns in France, Holland, and southern Germany welcomed the saint in various ways.

Midway in that period, Nicholas became the patron saint of Russia. It came about romantically in 987. Duke Vladimir, third in the dynasty of Russian princedoms, wanted to wed Princess Anna of Byzantium. Hers was a Christian empire, and before the marriage could take place, the duke had to publicly accept that faith. On their arrival into his city of Kiev, he made a proclamation that Orthodox Christianity was to become the religion of the Russian people. He brought from Byzantium wonderful tales of the saint and a fine icon portrait. The Russians

readily adopted him as *Nikolai Choodovoritz* (Nicholas, Miracle Maker).

One hundred years after the Russian episode, an Italian merchant ship from the port of Bari, returning from Constantinople with a cargo of grain and sixty passengers, became separated from its fleet during a storm. As it subsided they found themselves near Myra, and putting into port they went to the Church of St. Nicholas. The Italians had adopted the saint centuries earlier, and once inside the church four of the sailors, instead of just worshipping, decided to remove most of the saint's remains from the crypt—purportedly to save them from Saracens then raiding those coasts. When the ship arrived in the home port of Bari on the ninth of May bearing its sacred prize, there was cause for much celebration and ceremony, and the saint's relics were consecrated by Pope Urban. That same year a handsome white limestone church was begun, housing the crypt. Each year on May 9 a great demonstration is held in the harbor at Bari and within the church. And thus St. Nicholas of Myra is also known as San Nicola of Bari.

Earlier, the seafaring Normans, descendants of the Vikings, had conquered Sicily and moved up into southern Italy, some having been on the Bari adventure of 1087. From this and other voyages, as well as from returning Crusaders, they had learned much of the miracles of St. Nicholas. The Normans, in fact, had been his most active champions for several hundred years. A life of the saint was recorded in a book by a Norman monk named Jean in 1119, and there is the sermon-poem by Wace written about 1150. St. Nicholas appears in a play with music around 1200, both the work of a student of Abelard named Hilarius, and in a full drama of his life first enacted about 1300. By the year 1400 there had been five hundred hymns written to honor this favorite saint that were sung throughout all of France. □

The Gift Bearer

It was in France at the beginning of the twelfth century that bringing gifts in the name of St. Nicholas may well have originated. Nuns of the convents in the central provinces began the practice of leaving gifts secretly at the houses of poor families with small children on St. Nicholas Eve, the fifth of December. These packages, perhaps even stockings, were filled with good things to eat such as fruits and nuts and oranges from Spain, luxuries that would not otherwise have found their way into hungry homes. The custom spread rapidly into other parts of Europe and was soon being observed by rich and poor alike. In many communities on that same night, St. Nicholas Eve, a street parade was led by a man representing the saint himself, mounted on a white horse, dressed in a red bishop's robe and traditional mitred hat, and often carrying a shepherd's crook.

*A contemporary drawing (**above**) by James Lewicki illustrates the traditional Low Country wooden shoe with offerings for the saint's horse.*

*In northern European countries, St. Nicholas often delegated his unpleasant disciplinary tasks to a devillike aide—called Hansruhpart, Rumpaus, or Krampas. In this late eighteenth-century German etching (**right**), a hideously masked Krampas is at work while St. Nicholas stands by to come to the rescue.*

White Beard, White Steed

Until around 1300, the saint's beard had usually been pictured as dark. In its transformation to white lies a tale. More and more of his admirers began to see him as a version of Odin, or Wotan, the powerful pagan god of northern Europe. At the time of the Winter Solstice, December 21, when the sun at last begins to shine a bit longer, Odin could be seen riding through the night skies on a white horse, his long white beard blowing wildly in the wind as he led away the souls of those who had died that year. As Christianity spread, people preferred to think of those soaring souls as the angels of children looking down on their young friends. Children would leave at their doors shoes filled with carrots and hay for Odin's white horse, and by dawn the shoes would be empty.

In those days people could live on two sides of the same mountain or opposite sides of a wide river and yet practice different customs and speak different languages. But over many years these customs and languages might merge into one, or at least elements of one would be absorbed by the other. And so it was that St. Nicholas not only acquired a white beard but also a white horse for his mid-European visits. The function of the shoes did not change—but they were then to be found in the morning to be overflowing with good things.

18

Good Children and Bad

In due course, the saint's visit often was used by parents to exact improved behavior from unruly children. Some parents wanted only switches to be left for "bad" children—and many even wanted them applied! Clearly, such treatment was below the dignity of a saint, so in many regions he was accorded "servants" to perform disciplinary duties. Varying regionally, their names were: Hansruhpart, Rumpaus, Krampas, Knecht Ruppert, Ru Clos, Hanscrouf, Jan, Hans Trapp. They were menacing in their dark robes and hideous masks, some even horned like the devil himself. But St. Nicholas usually stopped his servant short of actual punishment by getting the bad children to promise St. Nicholas they would behave better in the next year. Then goodies were distributed, the kindly saint promising to return during the night with gifts for all.

Of course, there was bound to be some criticism of him and his ways, as spelled out in this verse by one Barnaby Googe (a possible forerunner of Dicken's Scrooge), in a book published in London in 1570 called *The Popish Kingdom*:

Another Krampas, this one with terrifying horns, in action (top) in a 1784 German drawing.

An old wood engraving depicts a typical street parade (above) held in many European cities on the eve of December fifth.

Saint Nicholas money used to give maydens secretlie,
Who, that he still may use his wonted liberalitie,
The Mothers all their children on the Eve do cause to
    fast;
And when they everyone at night in senseless sleep
    are cast,
Both apples, nuttes and pears they bring, and other
    things beside,
As caps, and shoes, and petticotes, which secretly
    they hide
As in the morning found, they say, that this St.
    Nicholas brought,
Thus tender mindes to worship saints and wicked
    things are taught.

Man of Many Names

The Dutch gave St. Nicholas a different kind of helper—sometimes three of them—called Black Peter or *Swarte Piet* or *Pieterman,* whose face and hands were stained black for the occasion. They were jolly fellows who often broke out in song despite the fact they carried switches along with the saint's bag of gifts. Their colorful costumes derived from the Moors, commemorating the end of Dutch troubles with Spain during the last half of the sixteenth century. The Dutch *Sinterklass* was even supposed to arrive from Spain, symbolized in a ceremony that is still carried out in the coastal towns of Holland to this day. He and his helpers, along with his white steed and their donkeys, arrive by boat a week or so before St. Nicholas Day. They proceed to the local city hall for the saint's speech and, during the next few days, make stops at factories and schools before visiting homes on the evening of December fifth.

To Black Peter was assigned the task of descending the chimneys that night, but gifts were incidental to the power this saint holds over every schoolchild, with recitations and drawings being presented throughout the year to their good *Sinterklass.*

Meanwhile, the Calvinist Protestants of northern Germany had insisted that gifts be brought as part of the celebration of Christmas instead of St. Nicholas Day. Here the elaborate ecclesiastic robes were shed for simple ones of fur with caps to match, and he became *Pelze Nicol* (fur-clad Nicholas), or in other regions *Buller Clos* (Nicholas with bells), or *Ashenclos* (Nicholas carrying ashes). In family visits he continued his talks about good behavior, though his role was now more that of a servant to the Protestant's *Krist Kindl,* the Christ Child, who to this day is represented as a young girl dressed in white and wearing a crown of candles. It was she who distributed the gifts.

The above was, and still is, true in northern Germany, but in other parts of Germany, St. Nicholas made his visits alone—and still does. He is known as Christmas Man *(Weihnachtsman)* or as *Schimmelreiter,* rider of a white horse.

Elsewhere today he is called by many names. The children of Belgium know him as *Sint Niklaes;* the Swiss know him as *Sant Nikolaus, Samiklos,* or *Santiklos;* in the lower parts of Austria he is *Niklo* or *Niglo;* on the tiny island of Helgoland in the North Sea he is their *Sonnerklas.* In the Tyrol he is called *The Holyman* and is accompanied by Saint Lucy, who distributes gifts only to the girls.

A wildly generous Pelze-Nichol (the fur-suited Nicholas), gift giver for Protestant Germany for hundreds of years, is portrayed in this 1890 print by Gustav Kuhn.

During the Twelve Days of Christmas, Britain's Father Christmas went from home to home, often on a white donkey, and even on a white goat. This drawing was done in 1836 by Robert Seymour, illustrator of the Pickwick Papers *in its initial serialization.*

The Boy Bishops

Tales of St. Nicholas's deeds and powers had been brought to England's shores by Norman sailors and returning Crusaders. Churches in many coastal towns were named for him—in fact several hundred by the year 1600. The ceremony of the Boy Bishops, recalling the teenage bishop of Myra, was practiced there even before 1300. A choirboy, elected locally on St. Nicholas Eve, took over most of the bishop's functions until Innocent's Day—three days after Christmas. In full regalia and with choir mates as his retinue, the lad would lead a procession from house to house, soliciting contributions by singing outside the homes of the well-to-do. This early practice of carol singing persisted for 300 years, until banned in 1645 by the Puritans.

St. Nicholas had no part in the feasting and general hilarity during the Twelve Days of Christmas until January sixth, Christmas Day of the old calendar. That role was filled by Britain's *Father Christmas* who, although he rode a donkey rather than a white horse from feast to feast, was often confused with St. Nicholas because of his red robe and white beard.

Known by many names and cast in many images, St. Nicholas now had been thoroughly absorbed into the cultures of western Europe. ☐

Father Christmas is celebrating with a group of mummers in this 1837 Seymour engraving from Hervey's The Book of Christmas.

2 St. Nicholas in the New World

Crossing the Atlantic

St. Nicholas was first carried to the New World on the ship *Santa Maria,* for it is Christopher Columbus who is credited with the first commemoration of the saint in North America. Columbus entered the Haitian harbor of Bohio in the West Indies on the saint's day, December 6, 1492, and to mark it he named the port St. Nicholas. But it was the explorer Henry Hudson who actually staked the saint's claim in North America.

Hudson was commissioned by the Dutch in 1609 to find a northwest passage to China. His explorations seemed to indicate that the rivers of the American continent were not the proper channels, but he brought back glowing reports of the lands he had claimed for the Dutch around the mouth of a river later to be named for him.

In 1621 the Dutch West India Company was formed, and gradually during the next five years many Dutch families were enticed with offers of land to settle in the New Netherlands. Then, in 1626, a whole fleet of ships loaded with settlers set sail from Holland, the lead ship, *The Goede Vrowe* (The Good Housewife), displaying on its bow a carved figurehead of their protector, Saint Nicholas. They landed at *Nieuw Amsterdam,* the little Dutch village at the southern tip of the island of *Manahatta,* which had recently been purchased for trinkets (valued at the famous $24 price) from the friendly Iroquois Indians. In gratitude for guiding them safely across the Atlantic, the settlers were said to have erected a gilded statue of their patron saint in the town square. Colonists from other European countries soon followed the Dutch, spreading their own cultures to the south, to the north, and eventually to the west.

Meanwhile, the stern puritans and the prim Pilgrims were colonizing New England and finding fault with all frivolities, especially in connection with Christmas. In 1651, the Massachusetts legislature passed an act ruling that *"whosoever shall be found observing any such day as Christmass . . . either by forebearing labor, feasting, or in any other way . . . every such person so offending shall pay a fine for each offense of five shillings to the county."* Thirty years later the ruling was rescinded, but many New Englanders never fully recognized Christmas as a holiday, except for religious ceremonies, until the present century.

Dutch settlers voyaging to the New World in 1626 as rendered in Our Country, *a 1901 history of the United States.*

Sancte Claus of Nieuw Amsterdam

New Amsterdam fell to the British in 1664 and became New York. The English who settled there, although at first unsympathetic to St. Nicholas and the innocent pleasure he brought the Dutch, were not so stiff-necked as their New England cousins. In their administration of the city they permitted the Dutch to keep their traditional custom of celebrating the Saint's Eve and Day on December fifth and sixth. The good hausfrauen baked their special cookies and scoured their homes from doorstoop inward to be ready for the visit of *Sinterklaas*, or *Sancte Claus*, as some children were calling him.

There can be little doubt that English children soon were begging to have the gift-bringer welcomed in their homes as he was by their Dutch friends. Nevertheless the process of shifting St. Nick's celebration from the traditional date of December 6 and the English date of early January to December 25 appears to have taken several generations to become fully accomplished. At the same time, it can be assumed that St. Nick was also taking care of New Jersey and Pennsylvania colonists from Germany, as assistant to *Krist Kindl* for those from northern Germany and as *Weinachtsman* for those from southern Germany or Austria.

Such an early Dutch cookie mold might have formed Sancte Claus treats of many shapes and sizes for children of old New York.

A modern interpretation of Saint Nicholas pictures him steering his white steed over old New York.

24

SANCTE CLAUS, goed heylig Man!	SAINT NICHOLAS, good holy man!
Trek uwe beste Tabaert aen,	Put on the Tabard,* best you can,
Reiz daer me'e na Amsterdam,	Go, clad therewith, to Amsterdam,
Van Amsterdam na 'Spanje,	From Amsterdam to Hispanje,
Daer Appelen van Oranje,	Where apples *bright*† of Oranje,
Daer Appelen van granaten,	And likewise those *granate*‡ surnam'd,
Die rollen door de Straaten.	Roll through the streets, all free unclaim'd.
SANCTE CLAUS, myn goede Vriend!	SAINT NICHOLAS, my dear good friend!
Ik heb U allen tyd gedient,	To serve you ever was my end,
Wille U my nu wat geben,	If you will, now, me something give,
Ik zal U dienen alle myn Leben.	I'll serve you ever while I live.

*Kind of jacket.   †Oranges.   ‡Pomegranates.

*This historic document in the story of Santa Claus was engraved in wood by Alexander Anderson as a memento to all members of the New-York Historical Society who attended the first annual celebration of the Festival of Saint Nicholas on December 6, 1810. St. Nicholas, or Sancte Claus, appears in traditional mien at **left,** but note the good girl and bad boy on the mantel and their respective stockings hung beneath—an overflowing one for the girl, but only a switch for the boy.*

NEW AMSTERDAM (NOW NEW-YORK).

*The New York skyline (**above**) appears here as it did in the seventeenth century before Santa was fully documented in the New World. It was over housetops such as these that his "coursers they flew."*

*A modern wood engraving of Washington Irving (**opposite left**) made by John DePol, from a daguerrotype in the collection of the New-York Historical Society.*

*A cartoon of the times (**opposite right**) shows Washington Irving conversing with his creation, Diedrich Knickerbocker, supposed author of* Knickerbocker's History of New York, *in which St. Nicholas was reported "laying a finger beside his nose" before becoming airborne.*

His Americanization Begins

The tasks of settling the New World were apparently too time-consuming and paper too scarce to spend much of either on such subjects as keeping records of Christmas and its frivolities, for little is to be found on the matter in Colonial literature. The small number of books printed concerned more serious themes: religion, the law, navigation, arithmetic, and the ABCs. But word about Santa did eventually get into the newspapers, as in this note from the *New York Gazette* of December 26, 1773:

> Last Monday, the Anniversary of St. Nicholas, otherwise called St. A. Claus, was celebrated at Protestant Hall, at Mr. Waldron's, where a great Number of the Sons of that ancient Saint celebrated the Day with great Joy and Festivity.

By the beginning of the nineteenth century, St. Nicholas had become an American fixture, at least in the New York area. This was to be officially recognized by the New-York Historical Society, which was founded in 1804. Six years later, on December 6, 1810, the society held its first annual Celebration of the Festival of Saint Nicholas. The early American wood-engraver, Alexander Anderson, executed a print for the occasion which was given to all who attended. It was the first known portrait of the saint to be made in America. A description of the sheet appeared in a newspaper account not long after:

> . . . a striking likeness no doubt, of St. Nicholas . . . holding in one hand a purse of money and in the other a birchen rod. In the background is a beehive denoting industry, and at his side a fine fat Dutch pug dog, the emblem of Fidelity. At the side of this *Goed Heylig Man* is a faithful reproduction of a warm, old-fashioned Dutch fireside on Sancte Claus morning. A brilliant copper Tea Kettle, a capacious Tea Pot, a plate heaped with waffles, and a Gridiron replenished with broiling sausages, presenting a pleasing prospect of the simplicity and comforts of the days of yore. The very andirons are in genuine Dutch taste: Two Mynheers smoking their pies and a pensive puss in the corner. On either side of the fireplace hang the Annual Blue Yarn Stockings. One, replete with Toys, Oranges, Sugar Plums and Oley cooks, the reward of filial respect and duty; the other containing alas, nothing but a Birchen Rod to castigate the refractory and disobedient. Over the mantlepiece is suspended an emblematic picture of the Good and Bad child. The smiling countenance of the dutiful daughter, whose little lap overflows with all that delights . . . is strongly contrasted to the doleful visage of the crabbed urchin doomed to wear the ominous Rod in his waistcoat button-hole on his attendance at school, an awful warning to his fellow pupils.

Washington Irving's Peculiar Fellow

The first written description of St. Nicholas himself to appear in America came from the pen of Washington Irving. Born in New York City soon after the revolution, of Scotch-Presbyterian stock, and named for George Washington, the young Irving displayed a restless nature. He left school at sixteen and tried studying law but soon gave that up to spend his days roaming the farms and forests and villages along the Hudson River above New York. These lands were largely populated by the Dutch, and Irving began poking gentle fun at these people in letters he wrote to *The Morning Chronicle* in 1802 and 1803, which he signed *Jonathon Oldstyle, Gent*. The New York newspaper was edited by his brother, Peter.

The popularity of his letters assured the young writer that he had the talent to amuse, and in 1809 he published *A History of New York from the Beginning of the World to the End of the Dutch Dynasty* under the name of Diedrich Knickerbocker. It was both a satire of the Dutch burghers and a spoof of that era's *Guide to New York City,* by Samuel L. Mitchell, and of the pretentious histories written earlier by Increase and Cotton Mather. *Knickerbocker's History of New York,* as it was soon called, was quickly traced to Washington Irving, and his reputation as author and humorist were firmly established.

"Knickerbocker" describes *The Goede Vrouw,* the ship which brought many Dutch settlers to New York in 1626, as being made "by the ablest shipcarpenters of Amsterdam, who, it is well-known, always model their ships after the fair forms of their country-women. Accordingly, it had one hundred feet in the beam, one hundred feet in the keel, and one hundred feet from the bottom of the sternpost to the tafferel . . . full in the bows, with a pair of enormous cat-heads, a copper bottom, and withal a most pro-digious poop!" He goes on to say that the "architect, who was somewhat of a religious man . . . did laudibly erect for a head, a goodly image of St. Nicholas, equipped with a low, broad-brimmed hat, huge pair of Flemish trunk hose, and a pipe that reached to the end of the bowsprit."

Irving told of the burgher's high regard for Saint Nicholas and of how the Saint would go riding over the house tops "drawing forth magnificent presents and dropping them down the chimneys of his favorites"—adding that "now he visits us but one night in the year when he rattles down the chimneys . . . confining his presents merely to the children." He also describes the hanging of stockings—"found in the morning mysteriously filled." But in the *first edition* (1809) no mention is made of the saint's flying horse, wagon, nor even his pack. In the physical description one learns, however, that the bishop's robes have been replaced by Dutch attire—"a low, broad-brimmed hat, a huge pair of Flemish trunk-hose and a (long) pipe." We will look again at Irving's book in its later, revised editions.

A Reindeer and Professor Moore

In New York City there was published in 1821 a small, sixteen page, paper-covered book titled *A New Year's Present for the Little Ones from Five to Twelve*. It was number three of a series of booklets called *The Children's Friend* and contained eight hand-tinted engravings. Despite its title, it was about Christmas and had many "firsts"—the first book on the subject printed in America, the first to picture Santa Claus in a sleigh drawn by a reindeer, and the first to mention gifts and the hanging of stockings at Christmastime. No author or artist was named.

Let's make a romantic supposition: Suppose that you lived at this time in New York and that you had at home some youngsters—and that you were something of a poet, though your occupation was that of a professor at a theological seminary. On an evening just before Christmas, you spy at a bookseller's that

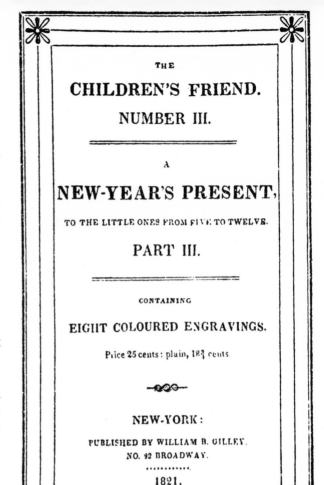

THE

CHILDREN'S FRIEND.
NUMBER III.

A

NEW-YEAR'S PRESENT,

TO THE LITTLE ONES FROM FIVE TO TWELVE.

PART III.

CONTAINING

EIGHT COLOURED ENGRAVINGS.

Price 25 cents : plain, 18¾ cents

NEW-YORK:

PUBLISHED BY WILLIAM B. GILLEY.
NO. 92 BROADWAY.

1821.

First American book about Christmas introduces "Old Santeclaus" as a gift-bearer and disciplinarian.

Through many houses he has been,
And various beds and stockings seen;
Some, white as snow, and neatly mended,
Others, that seem'd for pigs intended.

Where e'er I found good girls or boys,
That hated quarrels, strife and noise,
I left an apple, or a tart,
Or wooden gun, or painted cart;

To some I gave a pretty doll,
To some a peg-top, or a ball;
No crackers, cannons, squibs, or rockets,
To blow their eyes up, or their pockets.

Old SANTECLAUS with much delight
His reindeer drives this frosty night,
O'er chimney tops, and tracks of snow,
To bring his yearly gifts to you.

The steady friend of virtuous youth,
The friend of duty, and of truth,
Each Christmas eve he joys to come
Where love and peace have made their home.

6

No drums to stun their Mother's ear,
Nor swords to make their sisters fear;
But pretty books to store their mind
With knowledge of each various kind.

7

But where I found the children naughty,
In manners rude, in temper haughty,
Thankless to parents, liars, swearers,
Boxers, or cheats, or base tale-bearers,

8

I left a long, black, birchen rod,
Such as the dread command of God
Directs a Parent's hand to use
When virtue's path his sons refuse.

little book, *The Children's Friend,* glance through it, buy it as a stocking-gift for your six-year-old daughter, and go homeward.

Well, that did happen to a genial forty-three-year-old professor named Clement Clarke Moore. He lived outside the city's northwest edge in a fine home called *Chelsea House,* where he had been born on July 15, 1779.

The house had been built on ninety-four acres of land purchased by his maternal grandfather, Captain Thomas Clarke, a retired British Army officer. It

Old Chelsea mansion house

Clement Clarke Moore's homestead, Chelsea House, in midtown Manhattan, is where he wrote the famous poem and first read it to his children on Christmas Eve, 1822. This drawing was made by Moore's daughter, Mary, some thirty-five years later.

stood on a hill overlooking the Hudson River in an area that was later to become the neighborhood called Chelsea in the heart of Manhattan.

Clement Clarke Moore lived most of his long life there. His father, Benjamin, had been an Episcopal bishop of New York and, for ten years, president of Columbia College, from which young Clement was graduated with honors in Oriental languages. While studying for the ministry he compiled his *Compendious Lexicon of the Hebrew Language,* the publication of which brought him an offer that he accepted as professor of Oriental and Greek Literature at the General Theological Seminary.

All these scholarly pursuits may have influenced Moore to find relaxation in light verse and romantic poems, the practice of which helped him to win the youthful hand of Catherine Elizabeth Taylor, whom he married in 1813. Throughout their married life he composed many poems for her, and every family event for years to come found him bursting forth in verse.

By Christmas of 1822, six children had been born and Chelsea House was a lively place. They were: Margaret 7, Charity 6, Benjamin 4, Mary 3, Clement, Jr. 2, and Emily, eight months old.

" 'Twas the Night Before"

As Father Moore started off in the family sleigh on that afternoon of Christmas Eve for the nearly one hour drive to the Washington Market at the tip of Manhattan, he was calculating how big the turkey should be to satisfy the appetites of sixteen—counting household help of seven, including five slaves—plus energetic Grandma Charity. And he was also thinking of his promise to daughter Charity to write "something special" for Christmas.

That had been in his mind that morning as he and Jan, their man-of-all-work, a jolly, roundish, white-bearded Dutchman, had been clearing paths in the newly fallen snow. During the early-evening return from market, he relaxed as Patrick, the coachman, drove the horses pulling the well-filled sleigh through the whiteness under a clear sky. It all helped him piece together some lively lines of verse that were even then forming in this idyllic setting.

At home, the foodstuffs and gifts having been turned over to his Eliza, he sat down at his desk. And there lay the little book he had picked up a few days before. The opening page pictured a sleigh on a chimneyed rooftop laden with "rewards" and driven by an odd-looking, smallish saint. And pulling the sleigh was a single reindeer! Fine . . . but the moralistic tone of the later pages decided him against putting it in Charity's stocking.

But reindeer—that was a start! . . . and Jan, his old Dutchman of all work, seemed a perfect prototype for a really jolly St. Nick. Now where was it that he had recently read a Dutch description of the Saint? Yes, that was it! . . . in that amusing Knickerbocker's *History of New York* by his friend, Washington Irving, of which he had bought the third edition when it came out a few years before.

He reached for the two smallish volumes and, in thumbing through, hit on "Lo, the good St. Nicholas came riding over the tops of the trees." In short order, he made notes of all Irving had to say on the theme. He also recalled a verse on Santa he had clipped from the *Spectator* from some years before—and found it. He set happily to work . . . and had to be called several times before realizing that dinner was being announced as he was writing the closing lines.

As one account goes: He read the verses (see page 38) to the family after dinner. "Twas the night before Christmas and all through the house . . .''—and the children loved it, Charity begging that he read *her* poem again—and in the midst of the second reading they all laughed at little Clement having fallen asleep. And, though Eliza loved it, she probably made some such remark as "where on earth did you get such ideas?" Let us explore her query.

SPECTATOR VERSES, 1815

Oh good holy man!
  Whom we Sancte Claus name,
The Nursery your praise
  Shall proclaim;
The day of your joyful
  Visit returns,
When each little bosom
  With gratitude burns,
For the gifts which at night
  You so kindly impart
For the girls of your love,
  And the boys of your heart.
Oh! Come with your paniers
  And pockets well stow'd,
Our stockings shall help you
  To lighten your load,

And close to the fireside
  Gaily they swing
While delighted we dream
  Of the presents you bring.

Oh! Bring the bright Orange
  So juicy and sweet,
Bring almonds and raisins
  To heighten the treat;
Rich waffles and doughnuts
  Must not be forgot,
Nor Crullers and Oley-Cooks
  Fresh from the pot.
But of all these fine presents
  Your Saintship can find,

Oh! Leave not the famous
  Big Cookies behind—
Or, if in your hurry,
  One thing you mislay,
Let that be the Rod—
  And oh! keep it away.

Then holy St. Nicholas!
  All the year,
Our books we will love
  And our parents revere;
From naughty behavior
  We'll always refrain,
In hopes that you'll come
  And reward us again.

The Sources

Certainly that little book, *The Children's Friend*, had contributed the reindeer—and Moore's high spirits had dictated a *team*, though what pushed that number to eight no one has ventured to guess. The poem's meter may have been suggested by the verses in the 1815 Christmas issue of the *Spectator*, a form called anapests.

Irving's words had set Moore on his way to visualizing a new kind of St. Nicholas, and it is fortunate that he had not bought the first edition of 1809. In revising it, Irving had added much about the saint.

He had changed one of the four Dutch city-founders to a comic character. Fat Olaffe Van Kortlandt was made into a prodigious eater, sleeper, and sage who dreamed a dream in which St. Nicholas "came riding over the tree tops in that selfsame wagon wherein he yearly brought presents to children" and sat beside Olaffe under the tree where he rested. He "knew him by his broad hat and his long pipe and by the resemblance he bore to the figure on the bow of *the Goede Vrouw.*" St. Nicholas lit his pipe and *"the smoke from his pipe ascended into the air and spread like a cloud overhead."* It spread over the countryside, and Olaffe dreamed he climbed a tall tree and saw through the haze a vision of a great city with domes and spires. "And when St. Nicholas had *smoked his pipe,* he twisted it in his hatband, and *laying a finger beside his nose,* gave the astonished Van Kortlandt *a very significant look;* then remounting his wagon, he returned over the tree tops and disappeared."

Of the italicized words above, the only complete phrase Moore took was *"and laying a finger beside of his nose"*—though he wrote *aside of* for *beside.* From "the smoke . . . spread like a cloud over head" Moore wrote *"and the smoke, it encircled his head like a wreath."* "Gave a very significant look . . . then disappeared" became *"and giving a nod, up the chimney he rose."*

Portrait of Clement C. Moore (above), by Daniel Harrington shows him in his later years.

Fat Olaffe Van Kortlandt (opposite) dreams of climbing a tree and seeing a vision of a great city while little St. Nick calmly smokes his huge Dutch pipe. The early editions of Washington Irving's book carried no illustrations. This is the frontispiece and title page of the 1850 edition, with illustrations by F.O.C. Darley.

Squelching a Claim

For about forty years, beginning around 1900, a New York allergist, Dr. William Livingston Thomas (1871-1941) persisted in claiming that "Twas the Night before Christmas" (as he called it), was written by his great-grandfather, Major Henry Livingston (1748-1828), an officer of the Revolution. The family seat of the Livingstons was a large estate near Poughkeepsie, N.Y. The major, a dabbler in verse, never made the claim. And the next generation kept it pretty much to themselves, though stating that the poem first appeared in a Poughkeepsie newspaper around 1804-05 and that the manuscript was lost when one of the family's homes in Waukesha, Wisconsin, burned down in about 1847. Though he offered no proof, Dr. Thomas spent half his life in making the claim, receiving a lot of press coverage, and convincing many that it was impossible for the staid author of a Hebrew lexicon to have written such a poem. At no time has anyone squelched these claims by simply asking how those 1819 words of Irving's got into a poem supposedly written in 1804!

Moore's verses of St. Nick's visit would inspire literally thousands of drawings over the next 150 years. One of the first was this wood cut interpretation by T. C. Boyd in the 1840s. For more of Boyd's engravings, see pages 42 and 43.

"A Visit" Becomes a Classic

A few months after the first reading of "A Visit from St. Nicholas," Miss Harriet Butler, daughter of the Reverend David Butler of the Troy (N.Y.) St. Paul's Episcopal Church and a friend of the Moore's, was shown the verses by their "owner," Charity. She asked if she could make a copy. Miss Moore warned that the professor would not want the verses known as his. So when Miss Butler sent them to Orville L. Holley, editor of the *Troy Sentinel,* they carried no name. When they appeared in a newspaper just prior to Christmas of 1823, carrying the title he supplied, "Something About A Visit from St. Nicholas," the preferatory note said, in part:

"We do not know to whom we are indebted for the following description of that unwearied patron of children—that homely and delightful personage of parental kindness—Santa Claus—his costume and his equipage as he goes about visiting the firesides of this happy land, laden with Christmas bounties; but from whomsoever it may have come, we give thanks for it. There is . . . a spirit of cordial goodness in it, a playfulness of fancy, and a benevolent alacrity to enter into the feelings and promote the simple pleasures of children, that is altogether charming . . ."

Although in his verses Moore, perhaps because of his classicist background, chose to use the names *St. Nicholas* or *St. Nick,* the editor referred to this "patron of children" as Santa Claus, by then in common usage.

From then on the poem appeared constantly in hundreds of periodicals. Two early appearances were in the *Griggs Almanac* of the same year—both printed in Philadelphia in 1824. Its first publication in a magazine was in *The Casket, or Flowers of Literature, Wit & Sentiment,* Philadelphia, February 1826. A particularly notable printing was in the "Carriers Address" of the *Troy Sentinel* to mark the Christmas of 1830, for here it was illustrated for the first time. The wood engraving was by Myron B. King, and it showed Santa with sleigh and reindeer on a Dutch-American rooftop.

Not until 1837 did Moore allow his name to be used in connection with the work, when it was included in *The New York Book of Poetry,* and then several years later he even included it in his own volume of poems. The original manuscript of "A Visit" was not to be found when searched for in the 1840s, but there exist two known copies written out by the author at the request of friends. One of these has been preserved by the New-York Historical Society.

34

WE know not to whom we are indebted for the following description of that unwearied patron of children—that *homely* and delightful personage of parental kindness—SANTA CLAUS, his costume and his equipage, as he goes about visiting the firesides of this happy land, laden with Christmas bounties; but from whomsoever it may have come, we give thanks for it.—There is, to our apprehension, a spirit of cordial goodness in it, a playfulness of fancy, and a benevolent alacrity to enter into the feelings and promote the simple pleasures of children, which are altogether charming. We hope our little patrons, both lads and lasses, will accept it as a proof of our unfeigned good-will towards them—as a token of our warmest wish that they may have many a merry Christmas; that they may long retain their beautiful relish for those unbought homebred joys, which derive their flavor from filial piety and fraternal love, and which they may be assured are the least alloyed that time can furnish them; and that they may never part with that simplicity of character, which is their own fairest ornament, and for the sake of which they have been pronounced, by Authority which none can gain-say, the types of such as shall inherit the kingdom of heaven.—*Troy Sent'l.*

ACCOUNT OF A VISIT FROM ST. NICHOLAS, OR SANTA CLAUS.

'TWAS the night before Christmas, when all thro' the house
Not a creature was stirring, not even a mouse;
The stockings were hung by the chimney with care,
In hopes that ST. NICHOLAS soon would be there;
The children were nestled all snug in their beds,
While visions of sugar-plums danced in their heads;
And Mamma in her 'kerchief, and I in my cap,
Had just settled our brains for a long winter's nap;
When out on the lawn there arose such a clatter,
I sprang from the bed to see what was the matter.
Away to the window I flew like a flash,
Tore open the shutters and threw up the sash,
The moon on the breast of the new-fallen snow,
Gave the lustre of mid-day to objects below,
When, what to my wondering eyes should appear,
But a miniature sleigh, and eight tiny rein-deer,
With a little old driver, so lively and quick,
I knew in a moment it must be ST. NICK.
More rapid than eagles his coursers they came,
And he whistled, and shouted, and called them by name;
" Now, *Dasher!* now, *Dancer!* now, *Prancer!* now, *Vixen!*
On, *Comet!* on, *Cupid!* on, *Dunder* and *Blixem!*
To the top of the porch! to the top of the wall!
Now dash away! dash away! dash away, all!"
As dry leaves before the wild hurricane fly,
When they meet with an obstacle, mount to the sky;
So up to the house-top the coursers they flew,
With the SLEIGH full of Toys—and ST. NICHOLAS too.

And then, in a twinkling, I heard on the roof,
The prancing and pawing of each little hoof—
As I drew in my head, and was turning around,
Down the chimney ST. NICHOLAS came with a bound.
He was dressed all in fur, from his head to his foot,
And his clothes were all tarnished with ashes and soot;
A bundle of Toys was flung on his back,
And he look'd like a pedlar just opening his pack;
His eyes—how they twinkled! his dimples, how merry!
His cheeks were like roses, his nose like a cherry!
His droll little mouth was drawn up like a bow,
And the beard of his chin was as white as the snow;
The stump of a pipe he held just in his teeth,
And the smoke it encircled his head like a wreath;
He had a broad face and a little round belly,
That shook when he laughed, like a bowlfull of jelly.
He was chubby and plump, a right jolly old elf,
And I laughed when I saw him, in spite of myself.
A wink of his eye and a twist of his head,
Soon gave me to know I had nothing to dread;
He spoke not a word, but went straight to his work,
And fill'd all the stockings; then turned with a jerk,
And laying his finger aside of his nose,
And giving a nod, up the chimney he rose;
He sprang to his sleigh, to his team gave a whistle,
And away they all flew like the down of a thistle;
But I heard him exclaim, ere he drove out of sight,
" *Happy Christmas to all, and to all a good night.*"

N. TUTTLE, Printer—Office of the Daily Troy Sentinel—225 River-street.

The Troy (N.Y.) Sentinel, *which had launched Moore's poem in December 1823, also printed this illustrated version in 1830 as a "carrier's address," a single sheet which newspaper delivery boys handed out often for tips.*

*The earliest known color painting of Santa Claus is this
spirited 1837 interpretation* **(above),** *by Robert Walter
Weir, drawing instructor at the U.S. Military Academy at
West Point and a friend of Professor Moore. It now hangs at
the New-York Historical Society. Weir is grouped with the
Hudson River school of landscape painters.*

*Believed to be the first Christmas greeting produced in
America—and mistitled* Christmas Carol—*this version of
"A Visit..."* **(opposite),** *was printed in 1842 by the
stationer-printer, J. M. Wolff, of Philadelphia.*

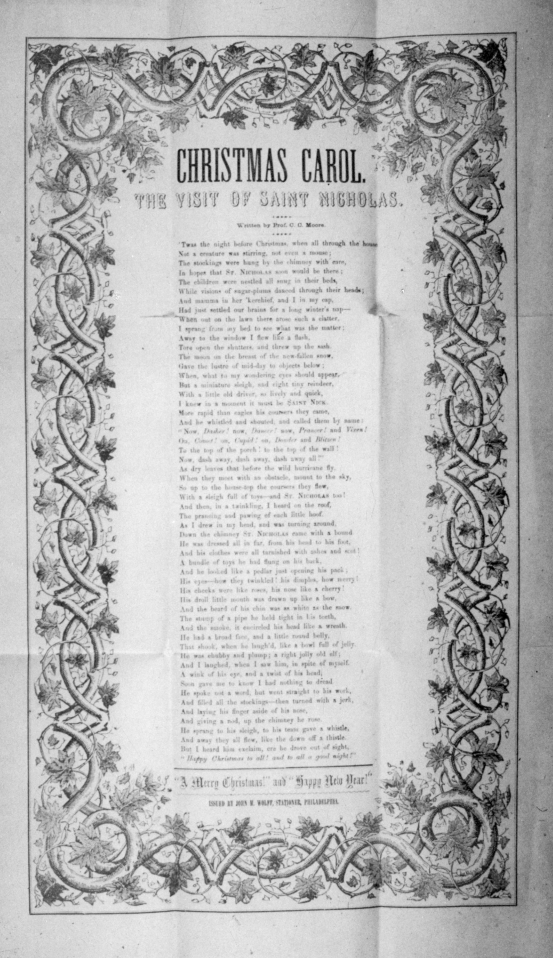

CHRISTMAS CAROL.
THE VISIT OF SAINT NICHOLAS.

Written by Prof. C. C. Moore.

'Twas the night before Christmas, when all through the house
Not a creature was stirring, not even a mouse;
The stockings were hung by the chimney with care,
In hopes that St. Nicholas soon would be there;
The children were nestled all snug in their beds,
While visions of sugar-plums danced through their heads;
And mamma in her 'kerchief, and I in my cap,
Had just settled our brains for a long winter's nap—
When out on the lawn there arose such a clatter,
I sprang from my bed to see what was the matter;
Away to the window I flew like a flash,
Tore open the shutters, and threw up the sash.
The moon on the breast of the new-fallen snow,
Gave the lustre of mid-day to objects below;
When, what to my wondering eyes should appear,
But a miniature sleigh, and eight tiny reindeer,
With a little old driver, so lively and quick,
I knew in a moment it must be Saint Nick.
More rapid than eagles his coursers they came,
And he whistled and shouted, and called them by name:
"Now, Dasher! now, Dancer! now, Prancer! and Vixen!
On, Comet! on, Cupid! on, Donder and Blitzen!
To the top of the porch! to the top of the wall!
Now, dash away, dash away, dash away all!"
As dry leaves that before the wild hurricane fly,
When they meet with an obstacle, mount to the sky,
So up to the house-top the coursers they flew,
With a sleigh full of toys—and St. Nicholas too!
And then, in a twinkling, I heard on the roof,
The prancing and pawing of each little hoof.
As I drew in my head, and was turning around,
Down the chimney St. Nicholas came with a bound
He was dressed all in fur, from his head to his foot,
And his clothes were all tarnished with ashes and soot!
A bundle of toys he had flung on his back,
And he looked like a pedlar just opening his pack;
His eyes—how they twinkled! his dimples, how merry!
His cheeks were like roses, his nose like a cherry!
His droll little mouth was drawn up like a bow,
And the beard of his chin was as white as the snow.
The stump of a pipe he held tight in his teeth,
And the smoke, it encircled his head like a wreath.
He had a broad face, and a little round belly,
That shook, when he laugh'd, like a bowl full of jelly.
He was chubby and plump; a right jolly old elf;
And I laughed, when I saw him, in spite of myself.
A wink of his eye, and a twist of his head,
Soon gave me to know I had nothing to dread
He spoke not a word, but went straight to his work,
And filled all the stockings—then turned with a jerk,
And laying his finger aside of his nose,
And giving a nod, up the chimney he rose.
He sprang to his sleigh, to his team gave a whistle,
And away they all flew, like the down off a thistle.
But I heard him exclaim, ere he drove out of sight,
"Happy Christmas to all! and to all a good night!"

"A Merry Christmas!" and "Happy New Year!"

ISSUED BY JOHN M. WOLFF, STATIONER, PHILADELPHIA.

A visit from St. Nicholas

'Twas the night before Christmas, when all through
    the house
Not a creature was stirring, not even a mouse;
The stockings were hung by the chimney with care,
In hopes that St. Nicholas
The children were nestled al
While visions of sugar-plum
And Mamma in her 'kerch
Had just settled our brain
When out on the lawn there
I sprang from the bed to see
Away to the window I flew
Tore open the shutters and th
The moon on the breast of th
Gave the lustre of mid-day
When what to my wonderin
But a miniature sleigh, an
With a little old driver, so
I knew in a moment it m

*Moore had many requests to write out his poem in his own hand; only two copies are known. The one **above**, the original of which has disappeared, was done for a friend named Chilton in 1856; the other, at **right**, was transcribed when he was eighty-two years old, shortly before his death.*

'Twas the night before Christmas, when all through
    the house
Not a creature was stirring, not even a mouse;
The stockings were hung by the chimney with care,
In hopes that St. Nicholas soon would be there;
The children were nestled all snug in their beds,
While visions of sugar-plums danced in their heads;
And Mamma in her 'kerchief, and I in my cap,
Had just settled our brains for a long winter's nap;
When out on the lawn there arose such a clatter,
I sprang from the bed to see what what was the matter.
Away to the window I flew like a flash,
Tore open the shutters and threw up the sash.
The moon, on the breast of the new-fallen snow,
Gave the lustre of mid-day to objects below,
When, what to my wondering eyes should appear,
But a miniature sleigh, and eight tiny rein-deer,
With a little old driver, so lively and quick,
I knew in a moment it must be St. Nick.
More rapid than eagles his coursers they came,
And he whistled, and shouted, and called them by name;
"Now, Dasher! now, Dancer! now, Prancer and Vixen!
On, Comet! on, Cupid! on, Donder and Blitzen!
To the top of the porch! to the top of the wall!
Now dash away! dash away! dash away all!"
As dry leaves that before the wild hurricane fly,
When they meet with an obstacle, mount to the sky;
So up to the house-top the coursers they flew,

With the sleigh full of Toys, and St. Nicholas too.

And then, in a twinkling, I heard on the roof

The prancing and pawing of each little hoof —

As I drew in my head, and was turning around,

Down the chimney St. Nicholas came with a bound.

He was dressed all in fur, from his head to his foot,

And his clothes were all tarnished with ashes and soot;

A bundle of Toys he had flung on his back.

And he look'd like a pedlar just opening his pack.

His eyes — how they twinkled! his dimples how merry!

His cheeks were like roses, his nose like a cherry!

His droll little mouth was drawn up like a bow,

And the beard of his chin was as white as the snow;

The stump of a pipe he held tight in his teeth,

And the smoke it encircled his head like a wreath,

He had a broad face and a little round belly

That shook, when he laughed, like a bowl full of jelly.

He was chubby and plump, a right jolly old elf.

And I laughed, when I saw him, inspite of myself;

A wink of his eye and a twist of his head,

Soon gave me to know I had nothing to dread;

He spoke not a word, but went straight to his work,

And fill'd all the stockings; then turned with a jerk,

And laying his finger aside of his nose,

And giving a nod, up the chimney he rose;

He sprang to his sleigh, to his team gave a whistle,

And away they all flew like the down of a thistle.

But I heard him exclaim, ere he drove out of sight,

" Happy Christmas to all, and to all a good night."

Clement C. Moore,
1862, March 13th originally written
many years ago.

NEW-YORK MIRROR.

A WEEKLY GAZETTE OF LITERATURE AND THE FINE ARTS.

Embellished with Fine Engravings, and Music arranged with Accompaniments for the Pianoforte.

FIVE DOLLARS A YEAR.]	SUBSCRIPTIONS RECEIVED AT THE OFFICE OF PUBLICATION NO. 148 NASSAU-STREET.	[PAYABLE IN ADVANCE.

VOLUME NINETEEN.	NEW-YORK, SATURDAY, JANUARY 2, 1841.	NUMBER ONE.

ST. NICHOLAS, ON HIS NEW-YEAR'S EVE EXCURSION, (AS INGHAM SAW HIM,) IN THE ACT OF DESCENDING A CHIMNEY.

In this number of the Mirror we had intended giving a Steel Plate engraving of Weir's celebrated painting of St. Nicholas, but were disappointed by the artist, and in consequence have substituted the Ruins of Carthage as this month's picture ; but, not being perfectly satisfied under disappointment, and having a very great reverence for the good old Saint who so often made our

tion to him. Yet how to do it half as well as our old acquaintance, Diedrich Knickerbocker, we know not, and must therefore turn to his authentic history of what was formerly called Manna-hata, then Nieuw-Amsterdam, and now Gotham, or New-York.

We find that after telling a great many goes on to say :

in the bows, with a pair of enormous cat-heads, a copper bottom, and withal a most prodigious poop !

"The architect, who was somewhat of a religious man, far from decorating the ship with pagan idols, such as Jupiter, Neptune, or Hercules, (which heathenish abominations, I have no doubt, occasio

New Year's Eve Visits

During the era of the 1830s and 1840s in and around New York City, the puritan attitude against any nonreligious celebration of Christmas was sufficiently prevalent so that many families had their feasting and gift giving on New Year's Day—following the visit of Santa Claus the night before. Both of the reproductions shown here carry dates and captions to that effect—and in the *New York Mirror's* issue of January 2, 1844, Moore's "A Visit" appeared with the opening words as "Twas the night before New Year . . ."—and ended with ". . . Happy New Year to all and to all a Goodnight." □

SANTA CLAUS,

THE NIGHT BEFORE NEW YEAR

Designed and Engraved expressly for the New Mirror by Sherman & Smith

For 1844

SANTA CLAUS

"A Visit" by Boyd

A friend and one-time neighbor of Moore, the bookseller-printer, Henry M. Onderdonck, in 1848 commissioned an elderly woodcutter, T(heodore) C. Boyd, to make six illustrations for a little sixteen-page paper book. This was the poem's first printing as a separate book. Boyd took literally the words "tiny reindeer," but (count them) he left out Dancer. This very rare and frail piece is one of only two known copies, both of which are in private collections (Melbert B. Cary, Jr., and Anne Lyon Haight). □

SANTA CLAUS'S

VISIT.

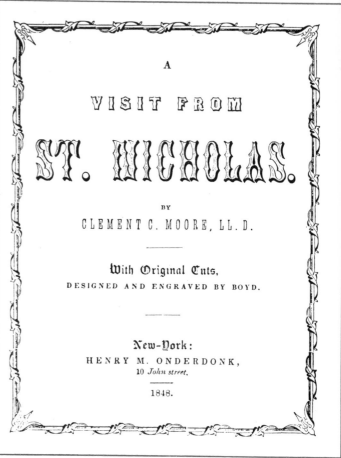

A

VISIT FROM

ST. NICHOLAS.

BY

CLEMENT C. MOORE, LL.D.

With Original Cuts,
DESIGNED AND ENGRAVED BY BOYD.

New-York:
HENRY M. ONDERDONK,
10 *John street*.

1848.

A
PRESENT
FOR
GOOD
LITTLE BOYS
AND
GIRLS.

VISIT FROM SANTA CLAUS.

'TWAS the night before Christmas,
  when all through the house
Not a creature was stirring, not
  even a mouse;
The stockings were hung by the
  chimney with care,
In hopes that St. Nicholas soon
  would be there;
The children were nestled all snug
  in their beds,
While visions of sugar-plums danced in their
  heads;
And Mamma in her 'kerchief, and I in my cap,
Had just settled our brains for a long winter's
  nap;

But I heard him exclaim, ere he drove out of
  sight,

"HAPPY CHRISTMAS TO ALL, AND TO ALL A GOOD NIGHT."

A VISIT FROM ST. NICHOLAS.

BY C. C. MOORE.

A cheerful Santa starts to emerge in this 1840 illustration **(above)** *of Moore's "A Visit..." in the collection,* Poets of America, *drawn by John Gadsby Chapman.*

Title page of a book–one of the earliest appearances of the name Kriss Kringle in print.

More Viking than saint was this Kriss Kringle-Santa **(below)** *appearing on the cover of* Harper's Weekly *for Christmas, 1859.*

About Kriss Kringle

The story of how the name Kriss Kringle became an alternative to Santa Claus, particularly in Pennsylvania, has some odd twists. You'll recall that North-German Protestants of the mid-seventeenth century had declared the Christkindl as the gift bringer, demoting St. Nicholas to the menial Pelze Nicol. That custom was followed by the early German settlers in Pennsylvania. But immigrants of the early 1800s, while bringing to America their Christmas tree and Christkindl, soon minimized and finally lost Pelze-Nicol (or Belschnicol). Then gradually, through intermarriage with the English, came progressive compromises resulting in the loss of the original meaning of Christkindl and in a figure resembling the Pelze-Nicol—but called Kriss Kringle—becoming their Santa Claus figure. However, gifts left by him for most young German-Dutch-English Pennsylvanians were to be found not in a stocking but among the branches of their Christmas tree. ☐

44

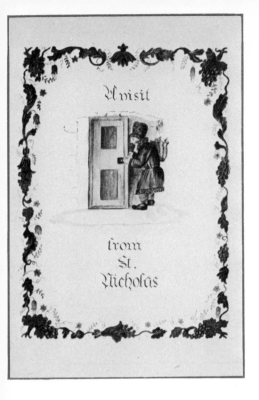

Mary Moore's "Visit"

[M]oore's fourth-born and third daughter, Mary, was a [tal]ented girl. Her older sister, Margaret, married Dr. [Jo]hn D. Ogden in about 1840. Soon after Margaret's [de]ath eight years later, Mary married the good doc-[to]r. As her Christmas present to him in 1855, she [m]ade the lovely sixteen-page book shown here in [pa]rt—the cover in actual size and some of the eleven [pa]ges with differing illuminated borders. Its frontis-[pi]ece was the drawing of Chelsea House, which has [al]ready been shown on page 30. □

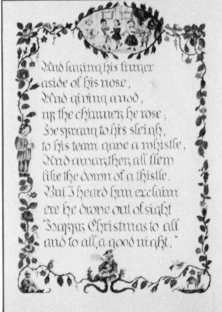

A fine illustrator of the mid-1800s was F. O. C. Darley, who drew this cover for a booklet of Moore's poem in 1862 *(above)* and this lively rooftop scene *(below right)* a few years earlier for Harper's Monthly Magazine.

Elfin helpers made their debut in the 1850 book, The Little Messenger Birds, where they serve a bossy Santa *(above right)*.

A happy Philadelphian Santa *(opposite left)* appears on a book cover; John Gadsby Chapman's book cover for A Christmas Book for All Good Boys and Girls *in* Harper's Weekly, *Christmas, 1859 (opposite right);* a young girl dreams of an athletic Santa dashing off to another rooftop *(opposite below)*.

46

More Early Santas

During the mid-1800s, there were many contributions made toward a developing image of Santa Claus—a few are shown here: the additions of a workshop with busy elfin helpers and jingle bells to the reindeers' harness, as described by Mrs. Caroline H. Butler in her 1850 book, *Little Messenger Birds;* some drawings by F.O.C. Darley that at the time were the best interpretation of Moore's Santa; and others as captioned. But it wasn't until the Civil War era that Thomas Nast began to draw the Santa version that was to become forever after associated in people's minds as Santa Claus. ☐

DREAMS AND REALITIES

SANTA CLAUS

THOMAS NAST—1840–1902

The great political cartoonist—and Santa Claus enthusiast—drew this pen-and-ink self-portrait when he was forty years old.

*One of Nast's earliest Santas, and first to be published in a book, was this fur-clad portrayal (**opposite**) illustrating the Moore poem in a 1864 book.*

Santa's Champion: Thomas Nast

The famous American political cartoonist, Thomas Nast, was born in Bavaria in 1840. He emigrated to New York at the age of six with his parents. Displaying a natural talent for drawing, he began his formal art education at age thirteen and made such swift progress that he landed a job on the staff of *Leslie's Illustrated Newspaper* just two years later. In another two years, he was selling sketches to accompany news articles to three periodicals, including the leading newspaper of the day, *Harper's Weekly*. Shortly after getting married in 1862, Nast went to Harper's full time. There his war cartoons were credited with gaining sympathy for the North. President Lincoln later said of him, "Thomas Nast has been our best recruiting sargeant."

It was in one of these war cartoons that Nast drew his first Santa Claus, or rather a man dressed and masked to represent him. Captioned "Santa in Camp," Santa is dressed in Stars and Stripes for this cover feature of *Harper's Weekly* of January 3, 1863. Inside the issue Nast drew small sketches of Santas with sleigh and reindeer as part of a center spread. And just before Christmas of 1863, another spread titled "Christmas Furlough" contained a close-up of Santa as a personality instead of as a masked man— and he was clothed in the fur suit of the Pelze Nicol that Thomas Nast had known as a child in Bavaria.

Nast later said that his annual making of Christmas drawings became a wonderful respite from his usual work throughout the year—his political cartoons that made him world-famous—for, though many were flavored with wry humor, few could be termed "happy," as are all of his drawings relating to Christmas and Santa Claus. On the following fifteen pages, sixteen of them are reproduced—about half of the total he made during the years 1864 to 1886.

Entered according to Act of Congress, in the Year 1862, by Harper & Brothers, in the Clerk's Office of the District Court for the Southern District of New York.

SANTA CLAUS IN CAMP.—[SEE PAGE 6.]

On the cover of Harper's Weekly *(opposite),* dated January 3, 1863, was Nast's first Santa Claus. Clad in fur-trimmed Stars and Stripes, he is dispensing copies of the newspaper as well as Christmas gifts.

In the same issue, the center spread *(above)* overflowed with wartime pathos, the only light touch being the Santa Claus scenes in the upper corners, enlarged **below** for a better look at Nast's first drawings based on Moore's St. Nick.

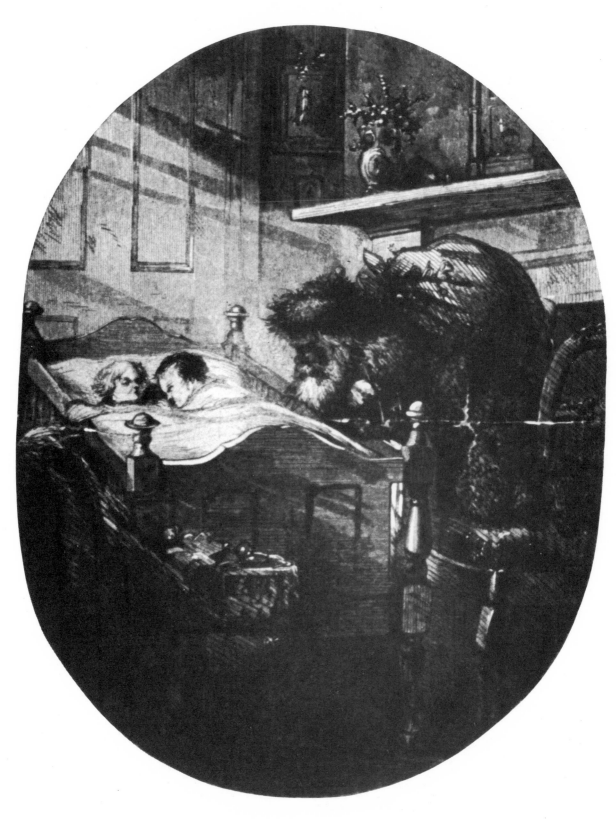

This enlargement from the Harper's Weekly *spread* **opposite** *shows Nast's first portrayal of Santa as a real person rather than as a masked man.*

A year after drawing the somber scenes on page 51, Nast came forth with this joyful spread for Christmas, 1863, in Harper's Weekly, *where the furloughed soldier returns to his family.*

THE SAME OLD CHRISTMAS

STORY OVER AGAIN.—[SEE PAGE 10.]

For the Christmas 1872 Harper's Weekly *Nast produced this triumphant array of characters from* Mother Goose *and other children's* **55**
stories being welcomed to these children's dreams by a rotund Santa in the foreground.

THE COMING OF

SANTA CLAUS.

A sleeping family's pets greet Nast's Santa Claus to a cozy parlor of the 1870s in Harper's Bazar.

Here is a potpourri of Nast Santas that appeared in Harper's Weekly or Bazar. The illustration of a youngster hanging a huge stocking **(opposite, above left)** was captioned, "...a chance to test Santa's generosity," in the December 30, 1876 Weekly. A two-page spread **(opposite below)** from the January 3, 1880, Weekly must have been much loved. One of the most popular of Nast's Santas, that appeared on January 1, 1881 **(below)**, is used on greeting cards even today, as is the Santa in the circle **(opposite, above right)** which appeared in a Bazar Christmas issue. Santa speaking to an enthralled audience **(right)** appeared in the December 31, 1882 Weekly and was captioned, "At the shrine of Santa Claus—we are all good children."

HELLO SANTA CLAUS . . .

. . .HELLO LITTLE ONE

Santa had one—but few others had a telephone when this spread ran in the December 20, 1884, Harper's Weekly. *The first experimental central office switchboard had begun operating only seven years earlier.*

Santa was indeed captured **(above)** *in Nast's* Harper's Weekly *cover for December 24, 1881.*

Nast's Santa paused for a relaxing smoke **(opposite)** *in the 1878 Christmas issue of* Harper's Bazar.

Nast scene **(opposite)** *of a boy and girl tracing Santa's route from the North Pole to the U.S.A. appeared in the December 19, 1885,* Harper's Weekly.

*Nast was his own critic. At first glance it would seem that this drawing **(above),** had been reproduced twice. Looking more closely, it will become apparent that after the one at **right** had appeared in print in December, 1870, Nast redrew it, mainly, it would seem, to make the young fellow and Santa more attractive.*

SANTA CLAUS'S MAIL.

An odd point in this Harper's Bazar *Christmas issue drawing is that Nast has the letters coming from the parents, not the children.*

CHRISTMAS-EVE—SANTA CLAUS WAITING FOR THE CHILDREN TO GET TO SLEEP.—[SEE POEM ON PAGE 4.]

In this Harper's Weekly *cover for January 3, 1874, without the explanatory caption, one might wonder about Santa just sitting there.*

"SANTA CLAUS CAN'T SAY THAT I'VE FORGOTTEN ANYTHING."

These two drawings were Nast's last for Harper's Weekly. *The young lady who is expecting an unusually large haul from Santa* (**opposite**) *and a peaceful rendering of "Not even a mouse"* (**above**) *were both from the issue of December 28, 1886.*

Nast's rich 1886 holiday spread for Harper's Weekly *was to form the basis for the color illustrations in the little book* Santa Claus and His Works, *which follow on pages 72-78.*

70

ACCOUNT BOOK.

RECORD OF BEHAVIOUR.

HOLIDAY WEEK.

MAKING DOLLIES' CLOTHES.

Birth of the Red Suit

Nast continued to contribute Christmas drawings to *Harper's* every season until he left in 1886, but probably most notable of these were the twenty scenes—seven of them close-ups of Santa—that appeared in the holiday issue for 1866. Here the jolly, rotund, gnomelike character acquired some new accessories: a long-range telescope for checking up on the behavior of children everywhere and an enormous record book of good and bad boys and girls.

Perhaps because of the good deportment theme, this spread proved to be so popular that *Harper's* could not begin to fill the many requests for extra copies. Nast was approached by the McLoughlin Brothers, publishers of the first children's books to be printed in a newly developed color printing process, with a proposal to redraw the seven close-ups in color for a book. This posed a problem for the artist, because he had always thought of the Santas he drew in black ink as wearing a tannish fur suit, which certainly would not contribute to colorful illustrations. The simple solution was to make Santa's suit in a bright red, and to add a little contrast he trimmed it with white ermine fur. Oddly enough, though Nast's name was widely known, it was not stated in the book, while the not-so-well-known name of the writer of the verse-story, George P. Webster, was given full credit. The book used the same title as the Harper's spread, "Santa Claus and His Works." Webster contributed the idea of Santa's headquarters being at the North Pole, which Nast had only inferred in one of the drawings. Webster's verses are on the next seven pages running beneath those seven Nast Santa pictures, which are reproduced here in about three-quarters of their original size.

71

McLOUGHLIN BROS., NEW YORK.

SANTA-CLAUS AND HIS WORKS
by George P. Webster

This nice little story for Girls and for Boys
Is all about Santa Claus, Christmas and toys.
So gather around me, but speak not a word
For I mean what I say, by you all will be heard.
In a nice little city called Santa Claus-ville,

With its houses and church at the foot of the hill
Lives jolly old Santa Claus; day after day
He works and he whistles the moments away.
You must know, he is honest, and toils for his bread,
And is fat and good-natured with nothing to dread.
His eyes are not red, but they twinkle and shine,
For he never was known to drink brandy or wine;
But day after day at his bench he is found,

72

For he works for good children hard, all the year round.
Though busy all day he is happy, and sings
While planning and making the funniest things,
Such as wagons and horses, and dishes and ladles,
And soldiers and monkeys, and little dolls cradles.
And garters and socks, and the tiniest shoes,
And lots of nice things such as doll babies use.
(See, the top of his head is all shining and bare—
'Tis the good men, dear children, who lose all their hair.)
With many things more, for I can not tell half—
But just look at his picture, I'm sure you will laugh,
With trumpets and drummers, farms, sheep, pigs and
    cattle,
And he makes the pop-guns and the baby's tin rattle;

Then he takes the new dolls that have long curly hair,
And, setting the table, seats each in a chair,
And he makes them pretend they are taking their tea—
He's the jolliest fellow you ever did see,
And can make a queer codger jump out of a box,
Or will make with his knife a new parrot or fox,
Or sit with his spectacles over his nose
And work all day long making little dolls clothes,
Such as dresses and sashes, and hats for the head,
And night-gowns to wear when they jump into bed;
With his dog standing near him, and spy-glass in hand,
He looks for good children all over the land.
His home through the long summer months, you must
    know,

73

Is near the North Pole, in the ice and snow;
And when he sees children at work or at play
The old fellow listens to hear what they say;
And if they are gentle, loving, and kind,
He finds where they live, and he makes up his mind
That when Christmas shall come in cold frosty December
To give them a call, he will surely remember;
And he's sure to have with him a bundle of toys
For the nice little girls and the good little boys.
Oh, if you could see him start out with his team
You would doubt your own eyes, and would think it a
    dream—

Wrapped up in a bear-skin to keep out the cold,
And his sleigh covered over with jewels and gold,
While his deer from the mountains, all harnessed with
    care,
Like race-horses prance through the cold winter air.
'Tis fun just to watch them and hear the bells tinkle,
E'en the stars seem to laugh as they look down and
    twinkle,
And the hungry raccoon, and the fox lean and shy
Give a wink as they hear him go galloping by;
For they know by his looks and the crack of his whip,
And his sleigh-load of toys, he is out for a trip.

Then the fox steals the farmer's old goose for his dinner,
Which you know is not right—but the fox is a sinner,
And his morals are bad and his habits are loose,
For he's never so gay as when stealing a goose.
Ah! here is a picture. Oh, children, just look
At the names of the good little girls in his book,
And a long list of names of the good little boys,
Who never disturb Pa and Ma with their noise.
There is Tommy, who tended the baby with care,
He gets some beautiful books for his share;
And Eliza, just think how bright her eyes will twinkle
When she looks in her stocking and finds Rip Van Winkle.
And Georgie, you know, is the five-year-old dandy—

Wont he strut with his pockets all filled up with candy?
There the old fellow stands with a queer knowing look,
Till he has in his mind every name in the book;
And he would be kind to them all if he could,
But he gives his nice presents to none but the good.
An army he gives to the boy who is neat,
And never cries when he wants something to eat;
And a farm to the boy who goes smiling to school,
Who keeps out of the mud and obeys every rule;
And all the good girls will get presents, we know,
And the boys who behave will have something to show.
When Christmas Eve comes, into bed you must creep,
And late in the night, when you all are asleep

He is certain to come, so your stockings prepare,
And hang them all close to the chimney with care,
And when in the morning you open your eyes
You will meet, I am sure, a most pleasant surprise;
And you'll laugh and you'll giggle and call to Mamma,
And keep up the noise till you waken Papa—
All of this for one morning will be very nice,
But the rest of the year be as quiet as mice.
How funny he looks as he stands on the round
And gathers the toys that hang far from the ground.
He is large round the waist, but what care we for that—
'Tis the good-natured people who always get fat.
The grumbling wolf who lies hidden all day,

And the fox that at midnight goes out for his prey,
And the serpent that hides in the foliage green,
Are all of them ugly, ill-tempered and lean;
But Santa Claus comes in his queer looking hat,
And we know he's good-humored because he is fat.
So when you grow up I would not have you slim,
But large round the waist, and good-natured like him.
Just think, if the ladder should happen to break
And he should fall down, what a crash it would make;
And that is not all, for besides all the noise,
It would frighten the dolls and would damage the toys.
I told you his home was up north by the Pole:
In a palace of ice lives this happy old soul,

And the walls are as bright as diamonds that shone
In the cave, when Aladdin went in all alone
To look for the lamp we have often been told
Turned iron and lead into silver and gold.
His bedstead is made of ivory white,
And he sleeps on a mattress of down every night;
For all the day long he is working his best,
And surely at night the old fellow should rest.
He uses no gas, for the glimmering light
Of the far polar regions shines all through the night.
Should he need for his breakfast a fish or some veal,
The sea-calves are his, and the whale and the seal.
Where he lives there is always a cool pleasant air,

Last summer, oh! didn't we wish we were there?
He's a funny old chap, and quite shy, it would seem,
For I never but once caught a glimpse of his team;
'Twas a bright moonlight night, and it stood in full view,
And, so you see, I can describe it to you.
See! Christmas has come, and he toils like a Turk,
And now the old fellow is busy at work—
There are presents for Julia and Bettie and Jack,
And a bundle still left on the old fellow's back,
And if Evrie behaves well and dont tear his clothes,
And quits teazing the cat, why he will, I suppose,
Find on Christmas a horse or a gun or a sled,
All ready for use when he gets out of bed.

But see he has worked quite enough for to-night,
He must fill all the stockings before it is light.
With his queer looking team through the air he will go,
And alight on the roof, now all white with the snow,
And into the chimney will dart in a trice,
When all are asleep but the cat and the mice;
Then will fill up the stockings with candy and toys,
And all without making the least bit of noise.
When the labors of Christmas are over he goes
Straight home, and takes a full week for repose;
And then when the holyday frolics are o'er,
He goes to his shop and his labors once more,
And all the long year with his paints and his glue,

He is making new toys, little children, for you.
So now I must leave you—but stand in a row—
Come Julia, and Bettie, and Louie, and Joe,
And Gracie, and Fannie, what are you about—
Get ready, I say, for a jolly good shout.
Now, three cheers for Christmas! give them, boys, with a
    will!
Three more for the hero of Santa-Clausville;
We know he is old, and bald headed and fat,
But the cleverest chap in the world for all that,
And a jollier codger no man ever saw—
But good-bye, merry Christmas, Hip, Hip, Hip Hurrah!

78

*In his final years, Nast returned to the Santa Claus theme in various media, including an oil painting of St. Nicholas holding the Christ child (**above right**) and a collection of Santa drawings published as a popular book of the 1890s (**below right**).*

With Santa Still in Mind

Following his abrupt departure from *Harper's Weekly* in 1887, Nast found it difficult to adjust from the hectic life of a news commentator and illustrator to a quieter one. Santa was still very much on his mind, so he persuaded *Harper's* to let him assemble a selection of his Christmas drawings for a book they would publish in 1890 titled *Christmas Drawings for the Human Race*. It contained dozens of them, many picturing Santa Claus, and was a publishing success.

Gradually he returned to the art form he had pursued as a hobby, that of painting on canvas in oils. Some of these paintings found their way into exhibitions as did the one at top right, which is one of his early Santas—Saint Nicholas with the Christ-child. ☐

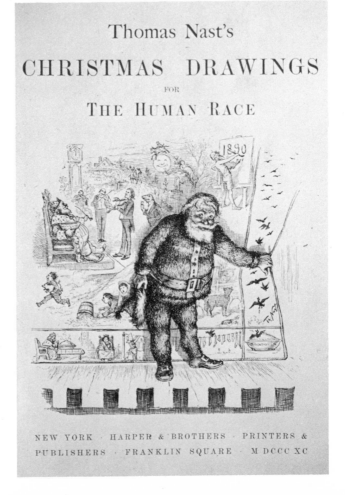

End of the Nast Era

Thomas Nast gave America several notable symbols besides his enduring image of Santa Claus. He was responsible for the elephant of the Republican Party and the Democrat's donkey; he dressed Uncle Sam in the Stars and Stripes Forever; and he created the Tammany Tiger which helped bring Boss Tweed's ring to ruin. His incisive political cartoons are credited with influencing the victories and losses of several presidential candidates, and one of them, Theodore Roosevelt, appointed him U.S. Consul General to Ecuador, where he died of yellow fever in 1902.

It took nearly a century and a little help from others, but three men—Washington Irving, Clement Clarke Moore, and Thomas Nast—are largely responsible for translating everyone's Saint Nicholas into America's Santa Claus, and for creating the model on which so many others would base their own interpretations. □

Nast's contributions to American political symbolism were enormous: here are his Republican elephant and Democratic donkey, a typical Nast cartoon, and the Tammany tiger.

3. America's Santa Claus

By the 1870s the Santa Claus we know today had assumed his hearty modern personality. But over the next hundred years, illustrators, cartoonists, and artists of all varieties would each put their own individual touch on the basic Irving-Moore-Nast concept. Santa would appear in magazines, hundreds of books, Christmas cards, on stamps and seals, billboards, handbills, in advertising of every kind. He would range in shape from elfin to obese, from stubby to lanky. At times, he would be off-stage, as it were, with the artist showing a child, waiting for him (see below). No matter what his appearance, his essence would shine through and his message would always be: "Happy Christmas to All!"

Prang's Auspicious "Visit"

Louis Prang (1823-1909), who later became known as the father of the American Christmas card, learned the craft of lithography in his native Germany, where it had been invented in 1798 by Aloys Senefelder. The technique of transferring impressions of drawings from stone to paper was still in its infancy when he arrived in New York in 1850. He moved to Boston to find work in his trade and set up his own shop there in 1860. In 1864 he created little booklets called "panoramas" for children. They were made by printing colors on one side of a sheet, trimming the sheet into long strips that were sewn end-to-end, and then folded like an accordian. The first so made was "A Visit from St. Nicholas" (without naming author or artist)—one of five such little books he called "The Christmas Stocking Series." Choosing "A Visit . . ." to start this new series could well have been inspired by his memory of the annual visit

An early winner in Louis Prang's Christmas card competitions was this charming girl awaiting Santa's arrival!

of Pelze-Nicol when he was a small boy in Germany.

By 1874, Prang had become widely known as the creator of the American Christmas card and initiated a series of prize competitions for card designs. The first competition in 1880 was limited to art students and offered four prizes totaling $2,000. Early in

1881, the contest was opened to all artists; in the competition that fall, the prize money was doubled, making a substantial sum for that era.

The resulting publicity not only spurred general interest in Christmas cards but stirred young artists to greater creativity. While Prang's name became

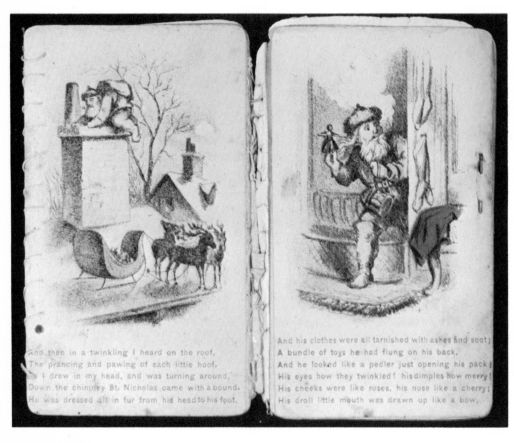

I knew in a moment it must be St. Nick,
More rapid than eagles his coursers they came,
And he whistled and shouted and called them by name;
"Now, Dasher! now, Dancer! now, Prancer and Vixen!
On! Comet, on! Cupid, on! Dunder and Blitzen, —

To the top of the porch, to the top of the wall!
Now, dash away, dash away, dash away all!"
As dry leaves that before the wild hurricane fly,
When they meet with an obstacle, mount to the sky,
So, up to the house-top the coursers they flew,
With a sleigh full of toys — and St. Nicholas too.

synonymous with the best cards of the era, he moved on to make his name important in artist's supplies, particularly in water color paints.

His contributions to several generations of Christmas card artists is well demonstrated on the pages that follow. □

s chubby and plump, — a right jolly old elf;
laughed when I saw him in spite of myself.
of his eye, and a twist of his head,
gave me to know I had nothing to dread;
ke not a word, but went straight to his work,
led all the stockings; then turned with a jerk,

And laying his finger aside of his nose,
And giving a nod, up the chimney he rose;
He sprang to his sleigh, to his team gave a whistle,
And away they all flew like the down of a thistle;
But I heard him exclaim, ere he drove out of sight,
"MERRY CHRISTMAS TO ALL, AND TO ALL A GOOD NIGHT!"

MERRY CHRISTMAS TO ALL AND TO ALL A GOOD NIGHT

Early Christmas Cards

Louis Prang of Boston introduced the Christmas card, and one of his first Santa cards is show below. But in these early years pictorial themes were generally flowers, bells, snow scenes, or various religious symbols. As the Christmas card caught on in the 1880s and 1890s—in England and Germany as well as America—portrayal of Santa became more popular as shown here, and on the following pages. ☐

*Santa Claus gradually became a popular subject for Christmas cards in the 1880s, some of which were printed in Germany. Typical of increasingly elaborate cards in the 1890s was this fold-out extravaganza (**above right**) with a tree-laden Santa in the window, a Christ child on the sill, and two pop-out children in the foreground.*

*In a Kriss Kringle card of the 1890s (**opposite left**), one sees features of both St. Nicholas and Santa Claus. By 1900, there were 1,330,000 telephones in the United States, and Santa, naturally, had one (**opposite, above right**). The finger-to-nose gesture of Moore's St. Nick (**opposite, below right**) was a recurring feature of turn-of-the-century cards.*

KRISS
KRINGLES

GREETING.

A merry Christmas

"THINE OWN WISH WISH I THEE"

Ellen H. Clapsaddle

Christmas Greetings..

Those Changeable McLoughlins

McLoughlin Bros. of New York published scores of children's books in chromo-lithography from the 1870s into the early 1900s. But they had some odd quirks. In their editions, not one artist was named—not even Nast for those Santas in white-trimmed, red-fur suits of *Santa Claus and His Works*. Soon after came many editions of *A Visit from St. Nicholas*—without naming Moore. The cover of one (undated, as were all their earlier ones) is shown at right with Santa in brown fur. At the top of the opposite page is a green-suited Santa on a book's front and back covers. In others shown here, he is in brown. Finally, in the mid-nineties, he got back his red suit. ☐

Six Nast drawings from Santa Claus and His Works *were reproduced by the McLoughlins for this cube puzzle of 1885.*

Of the many turn-of-the-century editions illustrating Moore's poem, *the two similar covers (**above**) had the distinction of changing the color of Santa's suit between printings.*

*This Santa/St. Nick book with a torn page (**left**) attests to heavy usage by young readers; a wild-eyed Santa (**below**) peers out of another edition.*

An Odd Santa Concept

These strangely-modern Santas are direct-lithographs from *An Adventure of Santa Claus,* Boston 1871, by its author, J. B. Greene. Eighteen others picture wild animals visited by Santa—and the facing pages of charming verse tell of this Santa (see below)—the son of ancient Odin. ☐

I.

Greet merry Christmas,—happy children all,
Let mirth and laughter ring throughout the hall,
Droop not in mourning for the dying year,
Which lends such heartfelt and such merry cheer,
In Arctic regions unexplored I roam,
Beyond the glacial ice-clad fields I come,
To join your pleasures in your happy home.
My father, Odin, northern God of War,
Repents the mischief of his eldest, Thor;
Bade me, his youngest, restitution make,
And from his store-house ample presents take;
With Cornucopiæ, and the Peace-pipe bring,
And add new pleasures and full anthems sing.

*An obviously non-Nast Santa graced the cover (**above**) of this 1875* Harper's Weekly.

*Mrs. Santa Claus made her first known appearance (**below**) in an 1889 book,* Goody Santa Claus on a Sleigh Ride, *by Katherine Lee Bates, who later composed "America the Beautiful."*

In a greeting card of 1885 appeared a lean Santa (left) drawn in the manner of Kate Greenaway; below left, a stumpy Santa of the 1880s has a relaxing smoke, and in an 1893 book, an unknown artist drew Santa (below) in the company of an elf and Mother Goose characters.

"MERRY CHRISTMAS," CRIED A QUEER SHRILL VOICE.   Page 84.

"OLD MOTHER HUBBARD" LED THE VAN.   Page 121.

The St. Nicholas *magazine cover* (**right**) *is surrounded by trade cards handed out by merchants. On the backs of these cards were Christmas greetings and often a brief advertisement as well.*

In the nineteenth-century, Santa Claus inspired various forms of popular music; note the unusually clean-shaven Santa **below**.

Magazines and Music

The *St. Nicholas Magazine* cover at left was for the December, 1874, issue, just six years after Mary Mapes Dodge (1831-1905), author of *Hans Brinker or The Silver Skates,* founded this beloved children's magazine. She continued as its editor for her lifetime, attracting most of the first-rank writers of that generation—Louisa May Alcott, Thomas Nelson Page, Rudyard Kipling, Mark Twain, to name but a few. In later years, another generation of authors included Faulkner, Fitzgerald, and Lardner, until it became a picture magazine in 1930 and expired altogether in 1940.

Santa Claus also inspired composers of popular music. Note the band music cover of 1867 above, and at right, sheet music for a quadrille featuring a fiddling and beardless Santa of 1846, drawn by one Spoodlyks. ☐

91

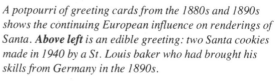

A potpourri of greeting cards from the 1880s and 1890s shows the continuing European influence on renderings of Santa. **Above left** is an edible greeting: two Santa cookies made in 1940 by a St. Louis baker who had brought his skills from Germany in the 1890s.

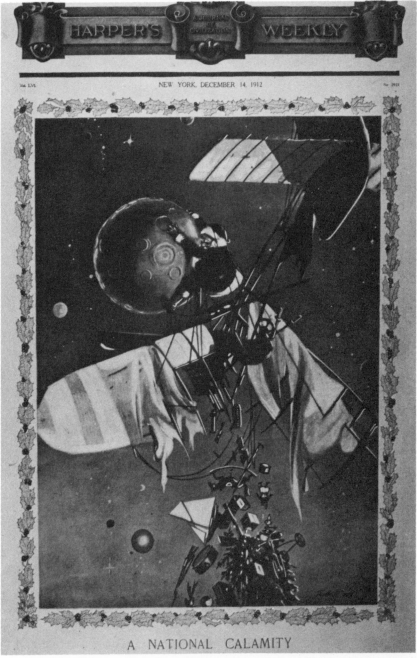

As the twentieth century opened, anonymous artists provided Santa with a variety of new means of transportation on trade and Christmas cards, including an airborne bobsled **(below)**, although on this Harper's cover **(lower right)**, Santa's airplane ride has proven disastrous.

A NATIONAL CALAMITY

SANTA CLAUS.

with him who did not come up the vines, who stopped closer to
the ground, for as soon as Santa Claus spied the two little fellows
asleep behind the chimney, which he seemed to do at once, he

94

An assortment of trade cards, greeting cards, and book illustrations of Santa by anonymous portrayers from the late nineteenth century includes a poster for St. Nicholas *magazine (1895) on which a bold highwayman accosts St. Nick* **(opposite, lower right);** *a dapper Santa* **(below left)** *checks out his list from a newspaper of the 1890s.* **Above** *and* **below** *are two chocolate molds of the same period.*

Jessie Willcox Smith (d. 1935), whose illustrations of Mother Goose, Robert Louis Stevenson's A Child's Garden of Verses, *and other classics have delighted generations of children, illustrated* 'Twas the Night Before Christmas *in 1912. Her rotund St. Nick, dressed in fur with fur tassels added, has had twenty-three printings so far.*

*A mid-European Santa about to visit a home from which the children peek out in anticipation (**opposite top**) is shown in a turn-of-the-century print.*

*A Dutch Santa (**opposite below**) leading a parade of children along a dike is depicted by the American artist, Edward Penfield, in his book,* Holland Sketches, *in 1907.*

The Great Illustrators

In the first half of this century many of the great illustrators of magazines and children's books tried their hand at portrayals of Santa, usually by giving their interpretation of the Moore poem. On the pages that follow are the contributions of Maxfield Parrish, N. C. Wyeth, E. Boyd Smith, W. W. Denslow, Jessie Willcox Smith, Norman Rockwell, Arthur Rackham, and a sampling of lesser-known artists whose Santas have graced magazine covers, posters, Christmas cards, advertisements, cartoons, and parodies of "The Visit from St. Nicholas."

*Painter/illustrator Maxfield Parrish (1870-1966)
gave his only known Santa Claus (below) a
wonderfully sweeping mustachio and a
magnificent plum pudding—along with a
characteristic Parrish hilltop castle in the
background—in this segment of a Christmas
cover of* Harper's Weekly, *1896. Parrish drew an
ascetic, cleanshaven St. Nicholas (right) for a
1900 edition of* Knickerbocker's History of New
York.

One of the greatest modern renderings of Santa Claus is N. C. Wyeth's masterpiece, Old Kris *(opposite), painted as the 1925 Christma
cover of* The Country Gentleman *magazine. Santa wears an 1870, Nast-type suit, but his jacket is a coat—and never has he carried
such a heavenly bag. As Wyeth did in illustrating so many classic adventure books* (The Last of the Mohicans, Robinson Crusoe, *and*
Treasure Island, *to name a few), he caught perfectly the central moment of the story.* Old Kris *and that one mouse still stirring are
occasionally shown during the Christmas season at the Brandywine River Museum in Chadds Ford, Pa.*

Santa with an Oz Look

Perhaps best known today for his illustrations of L. Frank Baum's *The Wizard of Oz*, W. W. Denslow illustrated the Moore classic in his own book published in 1902. In its introduction, Grace Duffy Boyland wrote:

". . . Those enchanting reindeer with their tossing, antlered heads and nimble feet are the hereditary property of every child in America. They belonged to the grandfathers and the grandmothers, and they will be the joy of the little people of the future since William Wallace Denslow has coaxed them into his pages and pictured them in his own delightful way for a new generation.

The model for Denslow's bouncy Santa might well have been T. C. Boyd's of the 1840s (see pages 42-43).

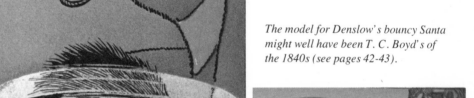

"It was certainly a happy thought to put the poem in a new and suitable dress and to embellish the lines with Mr. Denslow's whimsical humor. For it was written before it became the fashion to write down to children, and besides being a merry tale it is an excellent piece of literary work full of dramatic action and exquisite imagery." ☐

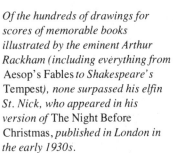

Of the hundreds of drawings for scores of memorable books illustrated by the eminent Arthur Rackham (including everything from Aesop's Fables *to Shakespeare's* Tempest*), none surpassed his elfin St. Nick, who appeared in his version of* The Night Before Christmas, *published in London in the early 1930s.*

101

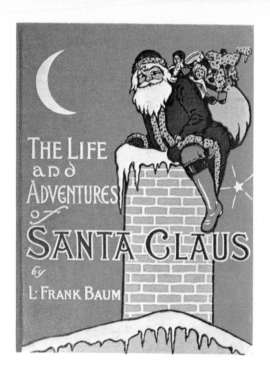

Baum's Odd Legend

L. Frank Baum was a New York journalist and playwright before he wrote *The Wizard of Oz* in 1900 as the first of his series of Oz books and the source of the classic film (1939) which perennially plays on TV, usually at Christmas time. Not as durable is Baum's own Christmas story, *The Life and Adventures of Santa Claus,* illustrated by Mary Cowles Clarke instead of his Oz-partner, W. W. Denslow (see page 100). Here is a summary of Baum's Ozlike version:

The Forest of Burzee is inhabited principally by woodnymphs of both sexes, ruled by AK, the Master Woodsman of the World. Deep in the forest, some nymphs find a tiny, human baby boy, bring him home, and name him *Claus.* As the boy grows, he makes friends with all others of the forest—the wood fairies, Jack Frost, and of course, the many wild animals—and takes as a pet a beautiful cat creature. Becoming adept with the tools in the nymphs' woodworking shop, he makes all kinds of wooden cats, including lions, paints them, and gives them as gifts, first to nymph children, then to human children outside the forest—but always secretly at night.

Soon a band of magical, evil creatures called *Angwas* try to stop his toy-making and gift-giving, but unsuccessfully. The Master, AK, takes Claus on a flying trip around the World. His forest friends and Prince Ryis of the Knooks then help him train deer to the harness and to fly—and is soon transformed into the gift-bringing Santa Claus we all know. □

102

Santa's Pre-visit Is Revealed

The artist E. Boyd Smith, who also wrote stories for children, created a book in 1908 with sixteen colorful pictures titled *Santa Claus and All About Him*. In it he told of something never before revealed about Santa—that he makes a pre-visit to observe people, children in particular, rechecking his lists so each boy and girl will get the most desired, or needed, presents. Of course Santa is invisible, except to the animals, who can't tell on him. He also visits the wild animals so he can describe them to his toy-making helpers. Back home, the giants do the heavy work, chopping trees for lumber, hauling in the boards as well as metals needed for toys. On his gift-bringing trip, Santa even carries Christmas trees, so his sleigh is heavily loaded indeed! *And*—he stays over until Christmas morning to peek in on the happy children. Then, it's back home for a big dinner and a long rest. ☐

Norman Rockwell, the great painter of America and Americans, put his Santa time and again on Saturday Evening Post *covers. Here are two of his earlier ones.*

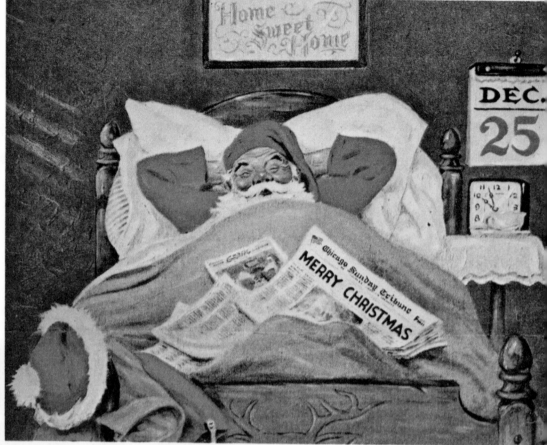

Santa takes a well-earned rest (**above**) as painted by Joseph Parrish for the cover of Grafic Magazine, of the Chicago Sunday Tribune, December 25, 1949. The cover of Esquire of December, 1946, expresses the childhood shock of Santa disillusionment (**left**), as drawn by Sheilah Beckett.

Opposite: above right is the cover, at **left** one of the illustrations, from Donald Duck and Santa Claus, a Little Golden Book, 1952; the drawings of Mickey Mouse as Santa were in a merchant's greeting booklet in the 1930s.

Esquire

THE MAGAZINE FOR MEN

ARTICLES
LOUIS UNTERMEYER
BROOKS ATKINSON
SIDNEY CARROLL
HERB GRAFFIS
JOSEPH E. SHANER
RICHARD JOSEPH
PAUL WILDER
HENRY W. HOUGH
FREDERICK PACKARD
JOHN C. ROSS
FRANCES GEIGER ADAMS
BILL GRAFFIS
SIDNEY FIELDS
MORTON BLOOM

FICTION
GERALD KERSH
JESSE STUART
GEORGE JESSEL
JOHN FREDERICK FRANK
N. O. YOUMANS
F. HUGH HERBERT
MEL MATISON
DRISCOLL THOMAS
RICHARD M. MORSE
THOMAS L. STIX

POETRY
WALTER BENTON

ART
E. OPPER
ALEXIS DE SAKHNOFFSKY
FRED ENG
B. SIMPSON
VAN KAUFMAN

ESQUIRE GALLERY
COBY WHITMORE
BEN STAHL
FRITZ WILLIS
JOE DE MERS
J. FREDERICK SMITH
EUCLID SHOOK
HARPER GOFF

PHOTOGRAPHY
WILLIAM STONE
ED RINKER
ARNOLD GLANTZ

SPORTS
ROBERT M. COATES
JIMMY JONES
ROBB WHITE
JIM CROSSETT

DEPARTMENTS
A. J. LIEBLING
JACK MOFFITT
O. E. SCHOEFFLER

CARTOONS
B. SHERMUND
D. McKAY

Donald Duck and Santa Claus © 1952 Walt Disney Productions

Donald Duck and Santa Claus © 1952 Walt Disney Productions

MERRY CHRISTMAS
from Mickey Mouse

Fun and Laughter with Santa

It is natural that, with Santa being so jolly, he is the butt of all forms of humor. The cartoons on these pages and elsewhere in this book need no explanatory words to bring forth a chuckle or two.

Walt Disney's Mickey Mouse and Donald Duck have always provided fun and merriment whatever their antics, and as represented here need no words to provoke a smile. Donald cavorting with Santa and Mickey's impersonation are but two of many Disney creations that presented the world's jolliest fellow on the screen, and in books for children of all ages. □

Merry Christmas from Mickey Mouse © 1939, 1938, 1937 K. K. Publications

Santa on Seals

Since the writer Emily Bissell created the first Christmas seal in 1907 to raise funds for the Delaware Tuberculosis Association, these bright embellishments of cards and letters have brought an advanced note of the holiday season. Over the years the National Tuberculosis Association and its successor, the National Lung Association, have put a Santa Claus theme on nineteen of the annual seals. And Santa can be credited as a supersalesman in promoting the cause of fighting serious lung diseases: a tallying of Christmas seal popularity indicates that Santa's visage usually increases the distribution of seals over the previous year.

For Christmas 1975, there were fifty-four different seals offered, each with a version of Santa designed by a school child from every state and U.S. possession.

Today in more than seventy other countries Christmas seals are issued to raise money for medical research and other good causes, and several are shown here. The U.S. Post Office hasn't recognized Santa's importance, having only once used his image on an official postage stamp; other countries, as you can see here, have been quicker to recognize his irresistible appeal. ☐

Below are Santas appearing on foreign seals. **Opposite: above,** *former U.S. seals;* **middle,** *the sixteen seals picturing Santa Claus drawn by school children in 1975;* **below:** *a strip from a block of 1976 seals.*

Santa's Rebirth in the Thirties

From the time of Nast up to 1930, we have seen how dozens of artists have portrayed Santa in a wide range of costuming and coloring and in all shapes and sizes. Then, in the weeks before the Christmas season of 1931, in all the major magazines of that magazine-reading era, on the billboards that looked down on roads and highways linking 5,000 cities and towns, and on retail counters wherever soft drinks were sold, there blossomed forth the heartiest, most universal Santa Claus ever. This brand-new Santa was promoting Coca-Cola. The reaction of the public was immediate and unanimous—they loved him.

He was just as he should be, jolly, roundish, ruddy, with twinkling eyes—as Moore had written:

> He was chubby and plump, a right jolly old elf . . .
> His eyes how they twinkled! His dimples how merry!
> His cheeks were like roses, his nose like a cherry!
> His droll little mouth was drawn up like a bow,
> And the beard of his chin was as white as the snow.

And yet this artist had given Santa something extra—he was human. What he had done was to take the Thomas Nast Santa and render him in living color, the only artist to succeed in combining the

*Haddon Sundblom, Coca-Cola's famous Santa artist, appears (**above left**) with the young model for his painting at **opposite left**. It is easy to see that he was his own model.*

*Santa checks his list of good boys and girls (**opposite right**) and on Christmas Eve pauses by the hanging stockings for a refreshing Coke (**opposite below**).*

110

Moore and Nast attributes and add an elusive plus!
(The artist also added a couple of feet to Santa's
stature. No longer was he the nineteenth-century
gnome, but now a robust figure standing close to six
feet tall.)

Haddon Sundblom was the artist. He was in his
early thirties and already highly successful as a
magazine illustrator and painter of pretty girls and
athletic young men in the advertising art of the day
when he took on the Coca-Cola assignment.

For the next thirty-five years at every Christmas
season, Sundblom would give the world a fresh view
of his marvelous Santa. At first, Sundblom recalled,
his model ''was a retired salesman named Lou Prentice, who embodied all of the features and spirit of
Santa Claus . . . the wrinkles in his face all seemed
to be happy wrinkles which were so evident when he
smiled and laughed.'' When Prentice died, the artist
searched far and wide for a new model but without
success. Finally a friend suggested that Sundblom use
his own face. ''As I took a closer look at my mug in
the mirror, I realized that I had there a cartoonlike
resemblance to Lou.''

For two generations of Americans, and for millions
upon millions all over the world, it is Sundblom's
Santa who is the real Santa Claus, whose face,
despite changing tastes and electronic times, radiates
the true spirit of Christmas. ☐

Rudoph, the Red-nosed, Makes the Team!

For the few who may not know the delightful tale of
Rudolph, the Red-nosed Reindeer, here is a briefing:
He was born with a huge, shining nose—the laughing
stock of all the other reindeer. One Christmas, Santa's trip was blocked by fog, so he enlisted Rudolph
to head the team and light the way, and many times
after he was called upon for that important spot out
front.

It was written back in 1939 by Robert L. May, in
verse form, for the mail-order firm for which he
worked. They published it in a paperbound edition as
a 1939 Christmas give-away . . . with illustrations by
Denver Gillen; two of the thirty-nine are shown here.
It has been republished many, many times since, and
Rudolph's name has joined the ranks of perennially
popular holiday songs. ☐

Other "Santas" in Other Lands

American children are far from alone in hanging their stocking for Santa to fill—for Santa has some active foreign counterparts. We have seen that he comes as *Sinterklaas* to the Dutch and that the English have *Father Christmas* to bring their gifts. In some parts of France he is called *Petit Noël* (Little Christmas); in the rest of France it is *Père Noël*—whose helper, *Père Fouchette,* carries the switches. In the Russia of today he is no longer The Miracle Maker, simply Grandfather Frost. Of course, the English-speaking peoples of Australia and New Zealand have their Father Christmas, but his get-up is more that of our American Santa Claus.

The Chinese, at least those who have left mainland China, have their *Dun Che Lao Ren*—meaning Christmas Old Man—and the children hang their stocking for him to fill. The Japanese man-of-the-season is a traveling-on-foot god or priest called *Hoteiosho,* who is said to have eyes in back of his head as well as in front in order to observe the doings of children—nonetheless he carries a big bag of toys on his back! In Brazil, the Portuguese-speaking children have their Papa Noël. In practically all Spanish-speaking lands, Christmas activities are strictly religious. St. Nicholas is but one of their saints. The children receive their gifts on January sixth (Epiphany). This is also true of Mexico, though our version of Santa Claus spills over their northern border to some extent. And among their hanging pinatas—which may take many shapes before they are broken with sticks to release the goodies inside—our Santa is often present.

Returning to Europe, the Scandinavian countries have their own diminutive, bearded gift-bringers. In Sweden there are the little Tomten, and in Norway and Denmark, the tinier *Jule Nissen.* These are all masculine, but in Switzerland it is difficult to tell the sex of their gift-bringer. It has a *Christkindl* look, white-robed and crowned, but with wings traveling in a sleigh that is drawn by six little reindeer that are ground travelers, not airborne like our Santa's.

The Italian people have had for a very long time a female form of Santa Claus—their *La Befana,* who carries a hand-bell to announce her presence, carries a sack on her back and a cane as a threat to bad children. She comes down their chimneys with gifts (and pieces of firewood for the very poor), but on January fifth, Epiphany Eve, from whence comes her name, Befana.

In recent years in these and other lands one may see not only traditional regional images of *Papa Noël* or *La Befana,* but the jolly visage of Haddon Sundblom's Santa as well—carried back via the worldwide distribution of Coca-Cola. ☐

*A modern rendering of Father Christmas celebrating with a group of mummers (**above left**) was painted one hundred years after its original engraving on page 22.*

*A Korean Santa (**below**) carries his gifts on his back in a wicker basket.*

The Strike of St. Nicholas

This parody, written by Louise Betts Edwards, appeared in the Christmas 1899 issue of the then-popular magazine *Truth*.

'Twas the night before Christmas, and all through our flat,
Not a soul was asleep, save the night-watchman, Pat.
The children sat up in their small folding-beds,
With grave intellectual doubts in their heads;
For though, half ashamed, they had hung up their hose
On the steam radiator—"Why, nobody knows,"
Said the dear little cynics, "if that old, ridic-
Ulous person exists, whom we christened St. Nick!"
So mamma, in her bloomers, was lurking in wait
To fill up the socks, if St. Nick, who seemed late,
Should fail to appear, when—heavens, the clatter!
We flung up the sash to look into the matter.
The arc light that streamed on the asphalt below
(The careful contractors had cleaned off the snow),
Showed—who but St. Nicholas, struggling to check
An automobile, in its pathway of wreck!
He whistled and shouted, in what I deemed Dutch,
Then dropped into English: "YES, THIS IS TOO MUCH!"
As the automobile, with a curve and a crash,
Struck a telegraph-pole, in a grand, final smash;
And the sleepy Pat Kelly was summoned to pick
Up the wide-scattered toys of the wrathful St. Nick!
His eyes, how they flashed! He looked far from merry;
His dimples were gone, and his lips, like a cherry,
Looked more like persimmons—the odd little elf!
I laughed at his anger, in spite of myself.
His heaving form shook like a bowlful of jelly,
As he viewed the poor toys gathered up by Pat Kelly.

" 'Tis my final appearance!" he cried, while, aghast,
The children looked on; "*positively,* the last!
For the sake of the youngsters, I've kept well abreast
With the march of the times, as your science progressed.
First, new-fangled heaters, that forced me to diet,
Down tortuous stove-pipes to crawl on the quiet;
Then, roofs so unsafe, with their angles and slopes,
I hauled up my reindeer with derricks and ropes;
And when you put steam-pipes in place of the stove—
A tax on my saintly endurance, by Jove!—
My old legs, lest the children their Christmas should lack,
Toiled up all your stairs with this huge pedler's pack!
I won't say a word of your spirit of doubt,
Though it's spoiled half my pleasure in going about;
For your twentieth-century world spins so fast,
My faith in myself is not fitted to last;—
But you clean off my snow!
                            And when I endeavor
By automobile to arrive, prompt as ever,
I'm ravaged and ruined, and routed and wrecked
By your telegraph poles, and, for once, *I object!*"
He shouldered his pack, whilst the children shed tears,
And called, in retreating: "Can't help it, my dears!
Go, publish the news in the press, if you like:
ST. NICK HAS GONE—ON A PERMANENT STRIKE!"
He vanished, his finger aside of his nose,
Unheeding a townful of ready-hung hose;
With sarcastic salute, as he faded from sight,
"Merry Christmas to all, and forever, good night!"

De Night in de Front from Chreesmus

Of the many parodies of Moore's "A Visit . . .", one of the most enduring and certainly the wildest is the small book written and illustrated by cartoonist Milt Gross in 1927. Here is a sampling—the first third of the dialect verses and a few of the author's more amazing interpretations of Santa:

'Twas de night befurr Chreesmas und hall troo de houze
Not a critchure was slipping—not even de souze
Wot he leeved in de bazement high-het like a Tsenator,
Tree gasses whooeezit—dot's right—it's de jenitor!
Hong opp was de stockings, site by site, Bivvy Dizz,
Lace pentizz, seelk henkizz; here witt dere a chimmizz:
Pricidding de Yooltite de ivvning it was—
Whan it gave on de durrbell de bozzer a bozz.
Und hout from de night wheech below was from Zero,
It gave hexclamations a woice "Hollo Kirro!"
I roshed to de durr witt a spreent troo de foyer,
Like hefter a hembulence spreentz it mine loyyer.
It was ronning from plashure all hover me teenges
Wot I pulled it durr hulmost huff from de heenges.
It stood dere a ront jost so high teel de durr-knob,
De faze fool from wheeskers and smooking a curncobb,
From de had to de hills sotch a werry shutt deestance
I navver befurr saw in hall mine axeestence . . .
De nose it was beeg like de beegest from peeckles
I weesh I should hev sotch a nose fool from neeckles!
De two leedle lags was so shutt witt so bendy—
Wot under de seenk he made sommersults dendy.
De belly poffed hout like a hairsheep a Zepplin
Und he wukked opp witt don like it wukks Cholly
    Cheplin.
So GEEVE a look! GEEVE a look!—GEEVE a
    look—QUEECK!!!
Geeve a look wot it's dere in de durrway St.
    Neeck!!!

115

"PASS ME LAST CHRISTMAS, WOULD YA! AN' NOW YA COME 'ROUND BEGGIN' FA PENNIES. TAKE THAT—YA BIG SWEDE!"

*This playful cartoon (**above**) by Percy Crosby appeared in* Life *magazine, December, 1926.*

*Santa rests while his elves read ''A Visit'' to him (**right**) in a cartoon drawn in 1956 by Ed Gunder for the* Associated Press.

An early riser announces Santa's visit in a cartoon by Carey Orr for the Chicago Tribune *(**below**).*

*A Turkish Saint Nicholas (**opposite left**) drawn by Thomas Derrick appeared in G. K. Chesterton's* The Turkey and the Turk.

*One of many fine drawings by Aldren Watson appeared on the cover of a 1945 book (**opposite right**).*

BREAKING THE BIG NEWS

A Visit From St. Nicholas

*One of but two Santas by Rockwell Kent (**below left**) was drawn for a friend's Christmas greeting booklet.*

*A modern Santa carries an overflowing bag of ''letters'' (**below right**).*

Santa and the American Christmas

The following is by the distinguished critic, author, and historian, Bernard DeVoto (1897-1955), from his *Harper's* column, "The Easy Chair," December, 1936, titled "Seed Corn and Mistletoe."

No one can approach through winter darkness a house from whose windows light shines out on the snow without feeling quieted and heartened. Psychic subtleties may be active in such a response, but there is no need to invoke them; for the obvious facts provide all the explanation we require. A house means warmth and shelter, light means human society. Snow and the dark have simplified the detail of the picture and deadened sound—they suggest tranquillity, which may mean much at the end of the day, and food or drink for restoration, and the talk of friends or family. The human mind is addicted to symbolism, and here is an image of ease, comfort, and reassurance that speaks directly to us in early childhood and from then on. . . . It is likely that very few people seeing a light on snow and quickening to the thought of warmth within pause to inquire whether the warmth comes from a gas furnace controlled by a thermostat or from the hickory logs burning on a spacious hearth to which a poetic sense would more properly attribute it. The light shining on the snow is quite as beautiful and quite as heartening when power to furnish it has been carried along a hundred miles of copper wire and stepped down through a transformer as when it comes from a candle dipped by hand.

Somewhere here is a text for a sermon, and sermons are appropriate to Christmas time, though with the clergy currently talking about a planned economy which will plow them under altogether, they may have to be preached by laymen. And everything about Christmas fares badly among the cerebral, who deplore its clearly reactionary nature, mutter about its vulgarization by trade and commerce, protest against its evil effects on children, and complain that it isn't what it used to be anyway and never can be again. Let us deal with these indignations first; for though the cerebral are always running a slight temperature on logical grounds, if the winter festival does indeed constitute a menace to society even a lay pulpit should take notice of it.

About the children. There are no statistical tables to tell us how many of them are still being deceived with an old and probably capitalistic myth called Santa Claus. Probably millions of them, for the mass of mankind has a gratifying disregard of theory, and parents continue, in spite of the heroic labors of educational psychologists, to deceive their children because they themselves were deceived a generation ago, remember liking it, and observe that their children like it too. The myth offends both a moral theory which holds that it is wrong to lie to children about anything and a highly scientific one which holds that you must not confuse a child's sense of reality by adding to his difficulty in dealing with real things the further difficulty of dealing with the altogether fictitious. Yet everyone knows that a child's sense of reality is quite incommensurable with an adult's and that children will make up phantasies of their own to supply the lack of any that may not be given them by others. The people who object to lying to children about Santa Claus must perforce lie to them about all the daily phenomena of existence, if indeed it is possible to say what a lie to a child is. And the very people who object to Santa Claus as a myth are prone to instruct them in such conceptions as human brotherhood, justice, and the classless society.

Both objections are on the level of the nostalgia which feels that the festival was all right for children when they themselves strung popcorn and cranberries to make decorations for the tree instead of the machine-made tinsel of to-day (but if that was Group Participation, was it not also Child Labor?), and that colored electric lights are tawdry whereas little candles once had a simple purity—it apparently being all right to burn the house up on Christmas Day so long as you keep the festival simple and pure. This is on the same level with that other sentiment of the thoughtful which sets out to make war impossible, along with racketeering and unfair competition, by keeping toy guns, cannon, and lead soldiers out of the hands of children. Beat the toy sword into a toy steamshovel, the notion goes, and you will turn the child forever to the ways of peace, at whatever cost of overproduction in the heavy industries. But if you do not permit the normal warlike phantasies of the child a normal expression at the right time you head straight for trouble. Either you will render him unfit for normal aggression later on, thus making him an easy prey for the combative, or you will insure such phantasies getting an abnormal and delayed expression, thus making war inevitable.

The unregarding behavior of untheoretical people is certainly sounder. They act on an assumption that the important thing is to make children happy. If you can give a child an experience of authentic awe and wonder and anticipation by telling him that a mythical fat man with a kind heart brings presents to children, why, the thing that counts is giving him the experience. If children like to play with toy guns, who is harmed? And if a child catches his breath in ecstasy because here in the living room stands an evergreen that has blossomed with colored lights, why that is everything in itself. You have given the child an experience of ecstasy, which needs neither justification nor analysis on logical principles.

One is constrained to be equally skeptical of the indignation that sees Christmas as a conspiracy against the public peace and interest by people who have Christmas presents to sell. Like so many other causes of the cerebral, this presents itself as a benevolent championship of the exploited, whereas it is really a contempt of the common man. It is the old, old cry of Utopians: the people are fools. The people, that is, are weak, gullible, infatuated, unstable, venal, too foolish to follow after righteousness—give us machine guns and we will make them virtuous. A cerebral dictatorship, ever so kindly but quite firm, would safeguard them from exploitation by the hucksters, defend them from the seductions of advertising, deliver them from the pumped-up hysteria of crowds. How pitiful that they should give one another presents because the department store tells them to, how intolerable that the System should make money from a sentiment that the people only think they feel! See how mechanically the common man jerks about on his wire and how slavishly he does what he is told to do by conspirators in the service of commerce. Therefore let us save him from himself, teach him that his emotions are not his own, and deliver him into self-knowledge and emancipation—at the point of a bayonet. . . . A lay pulpit must denounce all this fervor as propaganda—fascist or communist, whichever epithet will most affront the kindly theorist. It is an ancient despair uttering an ancient cry, the lust of the fretted to save the people by force. The people should ignore it altogether.

As of course they do. They go on giving one another presents at Christmas time no matter how the profits of the hucksters may pile up. They spend as much as they can afford to, and usually a good deal more. If trade prospers and the banks can express Christmas in the form of graphs,

the public is not appalled. Nor is its feeling degraded. The cathedrals of the age of faith, which the theories treat with the greatest respect, were fenced round by the booths of traders, and an earlier Christianity managed to combine a good deal of commerce with its devotion—and the roads to the American camp-meeting were thronged with peddlers whom the devout patronized without in the least diminishing their pious exercises. Not the trading booths but the devotion was the important thing about the cathedrals, and the important thing about Christmas is not that the people are sold presents but that they give them to one another. The most diverse and even the most irrelevant motives may enter in, many of them doubtless a good deal less than ideal; but the principal one, the one without which none of the others could possibly operate, is the human warmth of friends and relatives seeking expression and finding it. Christmas may be commercialized till it has become indispensable to the business system and vulgarized till a sensitive theory shudders when dealing with it, but people go on making gifts to those who are dear to them. The custom has the natural force of a stream flowing and takes its curve as a stream does, from its own nature. It is the popular fulfillment of human need and desire. The people behave that way, and you can do nothing whatever about them.

That is the firstly of a lay sermon. The secondly goes on to point out how, though in the American Christmas are recognizable many elements taken from many places, the whole is something altogether in its own terms. Our Christmas Eve is English and our Christmas morning looks very German. The carols sung in our churches and streets (and, to advertise soap or engine oil, in our broadcasting studios, a native touch probably loathsome to the sensitive) come from all over Europe but are French to a functional anthropologist, and medieval French at that. A good many of the conventional symbols are Asiatic, and the firecrackers which children set off in San Francisco and New Orleans exorcise demons and propitiate gods that are clearly Chinese. The mistletoe is Norse, and a vigilant suspicion, observing the holly and the eggnog, can detect compulsions bubbling in the blood of pagans far older than the rise of that star in the East which they are used to commemorate. Yes, a hodgepodge of rituals and symbols and of beliefs gathered at random, but it has taken a shape of its own which no one who has experienced it can ever possibly confuse with any other Christmas. One who has known the American Christmas as a child, a lover, or a parent knows a festival which has shaped his thought and patterns of emotion lying far deeper than thought, in a way uniquely its own. In whatever corner of the earth he may find himself on Christmas Eve, the rhythms pulsing in his nerves and the images translating them will have reference to the common and unique experience of Americans. That remembered, remembering child seeing the filled stocking and the lighted tree, hearing a Catholic carol so illogically sung in a Congregational meetinghouse, hurrying to deliver a holly wreath to a friend of his parents in order to try his skates the sooner on the ice of country pond or city sidewalk—is set off from all foreign children in things remembered and things experienced. An American tradition, different from all other traditions, has created its own symbols.

*Denslow's bouncy Santa (**below**) motions to his reindeer after one of his many visits.*

120

Children are going to believe in fantasy figures whether we adults want them to or not. With Santa, the discovery of gifts on Christmas morning is proof enough.

If a child is wavering, one idea is to explain that Santa is but the good spirit of Christmas and is never really seen, that visible Santas are his helpers who relay to him what everyone wants for Christmas. Children enjoy finding out that grown-ups can engage in fantasy and make-believe (as long as they don't overdo it). One psychologist says that belief in Santa lays the groundwork for a later belief in God—with which most clergymen will probably agree.

But all psychologists do not go for such ideas. One prominent man back in the midforties said flatly that *a child who is made to believe in Santa will have his thinking ability impaired if not destroyed.* There was a storm of angry rebuttals, letters-to-the-editor, fiery editorials, and even sermons. Apparently Santa fills such a basic human need (as did St. Nicholas) that it is wise not to attack him—at least not publicly!

If one wants to become scientific about belief in Santa, the Yale University Clinic of Child Development has reported that "most three-year-olds are aware of Santa long before they are aware of God. The four-year-old accepts every detail of the myth. The five-year-old embraces Santa's realism, clothes, laugh, and reindeer. The six-year-old believes with emotional intensity. The reflective seven-year-old has moments of skepticism . . . but adheres to his faith. At eight the notion of Santa is more etherealized. By ten, generally abandoned."

Perhaps, as your child reaches the age of seven to eight, it may be well to tell—or read out loud—the essential parts of the Saint Nicholas story and how imaginatively men made him into our Santa Claus. Then, when some smarty at school says, "I know something *you* don't know—there's no such thing as Santa Claus!", he will be prepared, and can tell the smarty the facts, that there IS a Santa in the best sense of the word. □

Seeing is Believing

If you are the parent of a small child, I hope this book will be helpful in explaining Santa Claus—if indeed it should ever become necessary. Most children just believe in him as long as they want. Take a child observing a somewhat seedy Santa at a department store entrance as he rings his bell to attract coins to a pot. Later, in the toy department, the child sees another Santa. One would think children would become highly suspicious, but most just accept Santa as a magical, wonderful man who can do *anything* —including being in two places at one time.

A detail (left) from the painting of St. Nicholas by Mainardi (right) reveals the saint's worldly sadness and pity. The painting now hangs in the Indianapolis Museum of Art.

Tarkington's Saint Nicholas

Booth Tarkington wrote this essay about his painting of St. Nicholas in 1945 for a friend, Earle J. Bernheimer, who issued it in manuscript form with a black-and-white reproduction of the painting. Only twelve copies were printed, so that few have seen this charming essay, "Christmas This Year."

Something more than a dozen years ago, at Princeton, I heard from one of the "Art Professors" that a painting by Mainardi, a fine example from the Florentine Renaissance of the high period, could be bought in New York for far less than its worth. The great Depression was then upon us; the picture had been put through an auction sale and a dealer had bid it in for a fiftieth of what had once been paid for it.

I went to his galleries; he brought out the painting and I stood puzzled before it. The central figure was that of the blonde Virgin enthroned and holding the Christ child upon her lap. That was plain enough; but who were the two tall saints flanking the throne? One, holding a book, was a woman, probably identifiable as Ste. Justina; the other one was the problem—a long, thin, elderly man, bearded, ecclesiastically robed, red-gloved and carrying four loaves of bread in token of what function I couldn't guess.

One thing was certain: this ancient gentleman was immeasurably compassionate. That was markedly his expression. A deep world sadness underlay the look of pity; he was visibly a person who suffered less his own anguish and more that of others. You saw at once that he was profoundly sorry for all of humankind.

When I had the painting on my own wall at home, I found that a gentle melancholy pervaded the room and the old saint seemed to add a wistfulness. "Don't you really wish to know who I am?" he inquired to me whenever I looked his way.

I did indeed wish to know him and to understand his sorrow, which was one of the kind we call "haunting"—all the more so because it was universal. Of all the saints, he was the one who most mourned over the miseries of this tangled world. We got out our books, wrote to iconographical experts—and lo! we had our man. The sad old saint is—Santa Claus!

He is St. Nicholas of Bari and his four loaves of bread signify his giving, his generosity. In time, as the legend grew and changed, the most jocund and hearty of all symbolic figures emerged from this acutely sad and grieving one. St. Nicholas of Bari became "Old Saint Nick," "Kriss-kringle" (a most twisted alliterative) and Santa Claus.

He, the troubled and unhappy, now comes laughing down the chimney, fat and merry, to be the jovial inspiration of our jolliest season of the year. We say that time changed him, made this metamorphosis; but it was we—"we-the-people"—who did it. Time only let us forget that St. Nicholas was a sorrowful man.

Mainardi put a date on the painting. It is clear and neat upon a step of the Virgin's throne—1507. In the long march of mankind, the four hundred and thirty-eight years that have elapsed since the Tuscan painter finished his picture is but a breath. St. Nicholas as we know him now, our jolly, shouting friend, a frolic for the children, may become the saddest of all the saints again, someday. What made us brighten him into Santa Claus was our knowledge that the world was growing kinder than it was in 1507.

St. Nicholas of Bari knew only a cruel world. Christmas of this year needs the transfigured image of him—the jolly one who is merry because the world is wise—and kind.

☐

Is Santa Still a Saint?

Over the years, I have been asked this question numerous times, and my answer has been a rather inconclusive: "Yes, I think so." In preparing this book I decided to find an authoritative answer. But first, let me quote from an article that appeared in *The New Yorker* magazine January 2, 1952—in the column, "A Letter from Paris," signed by Genet, who reported that, during the 1951 Christmas season, four powerful Roman Catholic prelates made "harsh denunciation of Le Père Noël, or Santa Claus." They characterized him as "a popular Canton-flannel lay competitor of the Churches' classically costumed Nativity figures, excoriated him as a Saxon myth who never existed except in parents' annual false-hoods to their children." Genet went on to report that "in Dijon, Père Noël was burned in effigy in front of the Cathedral Saint-Benique before the startled gaze of assembled parish youngsters . . . rousing unfavor-able repercussions . . . from newspapers, parents, and the four-and-five-year olds of the citizenry." That was in 1952. *What of today?*

To get an explanation I appealed to the director of the Office For Divine Worship of the Archdiocese of Chicago. I found that there had been no official ac-tion by the Church until 1968, so the Dijon episode of 1952 was a local action. He graciously responded as follows:

"The following is to help clarify the present litur-gical legislation regarding the Feast of St. Nicholas.

"It was not until the Middle Ages that the process of canonization was introduced into the Roman Catholic Church. A person canonized is formally recognized by the Vatican as a saint. This is pro-claimed by the Pope to the Universal Church so that anywhere in the world the person may be so vener-ated and regarded as a saint.

"It is important to keep in mind as a medieval process which is still continued until today. Before the process of canonization as approved by Pope Gregory (c. 590-604), there was no formal process, but persons were simply acclaimed saints by local communities or by public veneration. It would be true to say that none of the apostles were canonized. This in no way means that they are not saints. From earliest centuries they were venerated as saints. In certain locales, special days were assigned and the feast was celebrated; especially when local saints or early century saints were seen as special patrons.

"The recognition of sanctity either by a local community or through the process of canonization is quite distinct from celebrating the *feast* of that saint. I am sure you can understand that. The Roman Catholic Church at present has an official calendar which specifies the feasts of particular saints. This is a universal calendar for all countries and cultures and therefore is restricted only to those feast days that are celebrated universally.

"In the revision of the calendar a few years ago, certain *feasts* of saints who either no longer had a universal appeal or whose ethnic identity was not shared by other cultures or whose history was based more on legend than historical fact were removed from the universal calendar. This in no way denies the fact that they are saints and once were universally accepted and celebrated as a universal fact. This calendar reform does allow for more freedom. With less universal feasts, local customs, local feasts, saints with national or cultural significance can be given more particular attention.

"All this is preliminary to understanding the fact that the calendar reform of the Roman Catholic Church of 1968 *did not remove St. Nicholas* from the catalogue of the saints but did remove his *feast* from the universal liturgical calendar.

"Certainly, the history, stories, legends and tradi-tions surrounding St. Nicholas maintain his pre-eminence in the minds of christians as a saint rooted in a strong christian tradition. The calendar reform simply means that on December 6 it is not *obligatory* to celebrate the Feast of St. Nicholas according to universal Church law."

It is good to know that the ancient Saint Nicholas, from whom stemmed our American Santa Claus, may still be thought of as, and correctly called, Saint Nicholas and that celebration of his Feast Day on December sixth is entirely in order. ☐

"Yes, Virginia . . ."

Of all the images and words in support of Santa, no single statement has traveled as far and wide as the answer to an eight-year-old girl's question written to a New York City newspaper some eighty years ago: Please tell me the truth, is there a Santa Claus?

That was in 1897. The author was young Virginia O'Hanlon, who lived with her parents in a comfortable home on the northern edge of the West Side of Manhattan. Her father was a doctor and consultant to the New York City Police Department.

As she recalled years later, she was a firm believer in Santa Claus, who had been consistently good to her, but some of her young friends had started to sow the seeds of doubt. She asked her father for the facts. He was "a little evasive on the subject" but suggested she write to the Question and Answer department of the New York *Sun,* a leading evening newspaper in the days when evening newspapers were an important institution in a city family's life. Here is what she wrote:

Dear Editor

    I am eight years old. Some of my little friends say there is no Santa Claus. Papa says, "If you see it in the *Sun,* it's so." Please tell me the truth, is there a Santa Claus?

Virginia O'Hanlon

Virginia looked in vain for many days to see if her letter had been answered. The Question and Answer department had had the good sense to turn it over to the managing editor, who in turn had assigned it to Francis Pharcellus Church. Church had once been a Civil War correspondent and was then an aging and unknown editorial writer who frequently commented on religious topics, which he tended to treat with some skepticism. But on this occasion he rose to Virginia's challenge with this classic response which appeared as an unsigned editorial in the New York *Sun* of September 21, 1897:

"Virginia, your little friends are wrong. They have been affected by the skepticism of a skeptical age. They do not believe except what they see. They think that nothing can be which is not comprehensible by their little minds. All minds, Virginia, whether they be men's or children's, are little. In this great universe of ours man is a mere insect, an ant, in his intellect, as compared with the boundless world about him, as measured by the intelligence capable of grasping the whole of truth and knowledge.

"Yes, Virginia, there is a Santa Claus. He exists as certainly as love and generosity and devotion exist, and you know that they abound and give to your life its highest beauty and joy. Alas! How dreary would be the world if there were no Santa Claus? It would be as dreary as if there were no Virginias. There would be no childlike faith

then, no poetry, no romance to make tolerable this existence. We should have no enjoyment except in sense and sight. The eternal light with which childhood fills the world would be extinguished.

"Not believe in Santa Claus? You might as well not believe in friends! You might get your papa to hire men to watch all the chimneys on Christmas Eve to catch Santa Claus, but even if they did not see Santa Claus coming down, what would that prove? Nobody sees Santa Claus, but that is no sign that there is no Santa Claus. The most real things in the world are those that neither children nor men can see. Did you ever see fairies dancing on the lawn? Of course not, but that's no proof that they are not there. Nobody can conceive or imagine all the wonders that are unseen and unseeable in the world.

"You tear apart the baby's rattle to see what makes the noise inside, but there is a veil covering the unseen world which not the strongest man, not even the united strength of all the strongest men that ever lived, could tear apart. Only faith, poetry, love, romance can push aside that curtain and view and picture the supernatural beauty and glory beyond. Is it all real? Ah, Virginia, in all this world there is nothing else real and abiding.

"No Santa Claus? Thank God, he lives and he lives forever. A thousand years from now, Virginia, nay 10 times 10 thousand years from now, he will continue to make glad the heart of childhood."

*Virginia appears at age eight (**opposite**), the year she wrote her famous letter, and at seventy-seven (**below**), as Mrs. Virginia O'Hanlon Douglas.*

The *Sun* reran the editorial annually to introduce the Christmas season until the paper's demise fifty-two years later. Over the same years, the "Yes, Virginia" editorial was translated into at least twenty languages and reprinted by thousands of newspapers and magazines around the world.

Virginia O'Hanlon went on to become an elementary grade teacher in New York City schools, which she served for forty-seven years. In the final years of her career, she was assistant principal and teacher at a special school for chronically ill children in hospitals. As Mrs. Virginia O'Hanlon Douglas, she died in 1971. Over the years she recalled the *Sun* editorial as a high point and inspiration in her life and often said that Francis Church was the one who should be remembered, for it was he that "carried the philosophy of hope and love."

125

Finis

Acknowledgments

Acknowledgment of encouragement and help over the years in collecting and in visualizing this book is gratefully made by the author to: Rene Vaughal, Philip C. Duschnes, Walter Schatzki, and John Valentine (book dealers); to Ruth W. Jones, Martha Bennett King, Rubye Ingersoll, Anne Lyon Haight, Vincent Starrett, George Salomon; to William Cagle of the Lilly Library of the University of Indiana (for special favors); and to my son, David W. Jones, who priorly made over one hundred of the photo copies used herein from material in my collection.

Grateful acknowledgment is made to the following persons and organizations for permission to reproduce the following illustrative material. Unless otherwise indicated, the works are from the collection of the author. **4-5:** Rainey Bennett; **6:** Scala; **7 top:** The Metropolitan Museum of Art, New York. Gift of Coudert Brothers, 1888; **9 top**: Scala; **10 top**: The Metropolitan Museum of Art, New York. Gift of Francis Kleinberger, 1916; **10 bottom**: Scala; **13**: The Metropolitan Museum of Art, New York. The Cloisters Collection, Purchase, 1954; **16 left**: Middle Eastern Technical University, Ankara; **16 right**: Turkish Information Office; **18**: James Lewicki; **24 right**: Rainey Bennett; **25**: The New-York Historical Society; **27 top**: The Bettmann Archive; **33, 35, 36**: The New-York Historical Society; **44 top left and bottom right**: Pennsylvania State University Libraries; **94 bottom right**: Willis M. Ravinus; **95 top right**: Robert Frerck; **95 bottom right**: Mr. and Mrs. Ralph F. Huck; **96 bottom**: Original illustration by Edward Penfield from *Holland Sketches* by Edward Penfield. Used by permission of Charles Scribner's Sons; **97**: Original illustration by Jessie Willcox Smith from *'Twas the Night Before Christmas* by Clement C. Moore. Used by permission of Houghton Mifflin Company; **99**: Photograph courtesy of the Brandywine River Museum; **101**: Barbara Edwards; **103**: From *Santa Claus and All About Him* by E. Boyd Smith. Copyright 1908, renewed 1936 by E. Boyd Smith. Reproduced by permission of J. B. Lippincott Company; **104**: Reprinted by permission from *The Saturday Evening Post* ©1922 The Curtis Publishing Company; **105**: Reprinted with permission from *The Saturday Evening Post* ©1926 The Curtis Publishing Company; **106 top**: Reprinted, courtesy of The Chicago Tribune; **106 bottom**: Reprinted by permission of Esquire Magazine ©1946 by Esquire Inc.; **109**: American Lung Association; **110 top**: The Chicago Tribune; **110, 111, 112 left**: Courtesy, The Archives, The Coca-Cola Company, Atlanta, Georgia; **112 top right and bottom right**: Original illustrations by Denver Gillen from *Rudolph the Red-Nosed Reindeer* by Robert L. May. Copyright 1939 by Robert L. May. Used by permission of Follett Publishing Company; **113 left**: Original illustration by Relf from The Bystander magazine, November 1937; **115**: Excerpt from *De Night in De Front from Chreesmas* by Milt Gross. Copyright 1927 by George H. Doran Company; **116 top**: Henry T. Rockwell; **116 middle**: Associated Press; **116 bottom**: Reprinted, courtesy of The Chicago Tribune; **117 bottom left**: Rockwell Kent Legacies; **117 top right**: Peter Pauper Press; **117 bottom right**: Bauer Alphabets; **118 illustration**: Brinton Turkle; **118 text** ©1936 Bernard DeVoto. Reprinted with permission; **122 art**: Indianapolis Museum of Art; **122 text**: Booth Tarkington Estate; **124, 125**: *The Chicago Sun-Times*.